VOLUNTARY RETIREMENT-SERVICE MATTERS-SUPREME COURT'S LATEST LEADING CASE LAWS

CASE NOTES- FACTS- FINDINGS OF APEX COURT JUDGES & CITATIONS

JAYPRAKASH BANSILAL SOMANI

ISBN 979-888569156-7

Dedicated

To

All the Past & Present Judges of the Supreme Court of India.

Salute to their wisdom.

Salute to their interpretation of Law.

Salute to their elaborative judgement writing.

ꕤ

Contents

Preface *vii*

Acknowledgements *ix*

1. Indian Bank And Ors. Vs. Mahaveer Khariwal, 2021 1
2. New Victoria Mills And Ors. Vs. Shrikant Arya, 2021 5
3. Union Of India (uoi) And Ors. Vs. Abhiram Verma, 2021 7
4. Rajasthan State Road Transport Corporation Ltd. And Ors. Vs. Mohani Devi And Ors., 2020 10
5. Assistant General Manager And Ors. Vs. Radhey Shyam Pandey, 2020 14
6. Karan Singh Vs. Delhi Transport Corporation And Ors., 2019 19
7. State Of West Bengal And Ors. Vs. Tonmoy Mondal, 2019 22
8. Central Bank Of India And Ors. Vs. Tara Chand, 2019 26
9. State Of Uttar Pradesh And Ors. Vs. Achal Singh, 2018 29
10. State Bank Of Patiala And Ors. Vs. Kanwal Nain Singh, 2018 32
11. National Insurance Special Voluntary Retired/retired Employees Association And Ors. Vs. United India Insurance Co. Ltd. And Ors., 2018 34
12. Surjeet Singh Bhamra Vs. Bank Of India And Ors., 2016 37
13. Madhya Pradesh State Road Transport Corporation Vs. Manoj Kumar And Ors., 2016 40
14. Assistant General Manager, State Bank Of India And Ors. Vs. Radhey Shyam Pandey And Ors., 2015 44
15. Senior Divisional Manager Life Insurance Corporation Of India Ltd. And Ors. Vs. Lal Meena, 2015 49
16. Exide Industries Ltd. Vs. Union Of India (uoi) And Ors., 2015 52
17. P. Krishna Murthy Vs. The Commissioner Of Sericulture Andhra Pradesh, 2014 55
18. State Of Bank Of Patiala Vs. Pritam Singh Bedi, 2014 58
19. Union Of India (uoi) And Ors. Vs. Ajay Wahi 61

Contents

20. M.d. Orissa S.h.w. Coop. Sty. Ltd. Vs. Satyanarayan Pattnaik And Ors., 2014 64

Videos & Tv Shows On Law & Exim 67

List Of Adv. Jayprakash Somani's Books 73

Preface

Dear Learned Advocates of the Trial Courts, Tribunals, Appellate Tribunals, High Courts, Supreme Court, HR Professionals, Corporates, Govt Recruitment Officers & Employees,

I am very delighted to provide you a book on 'Voluntary Retirement - Service Matters' - Supreme Court of India's Latest Leading Case Laws'.

In this book you will get...

1. Name of the Case i. e. Cause title

2.Relevant Sections discussed in the case

3.Hon'ble Judges/Coram of the case

4.Number of PDF Pages in Original Judgement of the case

5. All available Citations of the case

6. Case Note with appeal allowed/ dismissed or disposed off

7. Facts of the case

8.Hon'ble Apex Court's findings, while dismissing/allowing or disposing the appeal

9. Ratio Decidendi if any.

My special thanks to Manupatra, because of their web portal I can compile this book in well manner. I am also thankful to Notion Press to support me to publish & market this book throughout the Country. Thanks to my Juniors, Advocate Colleagues & Insolvency Professional Colleagues to support me in this venture.

Miss Devpriya Shah has helped me a lot to compile this book.

I hope this book will add some value addition in the wealth of your legal knowledge. Your positive feedbacks will boost me to compile/ write further books & negative feedbacks will improve my skills. Kindly send your valuable feedbacks by email.

Thanks with Regards,

Jayprakash B. Somani

Advocate, Supreme Court of India

Email: jaysomani64@gmail.com

Web Site:www.jayprakashsomani.com

Call: 8384051134, 9322188701, 9318381287

ACKNOWLEDGEMENTS

Printed & Published by
Notion Press
No. 8, 3rd Cross Street,
CIT Colony, Mylapore,
Chennai, Tamil Nadu- 600004

Managed by
Jayprakash Somani Advocates & Solicitors
Law Firm for Supreme Court of India
Delhi Office
257 C, Pocket 1, Mayur Vihar Phase 1, Delhi 110091.
Call 8384051134, 9322188701, 8459194576, 01141051516
Supreme Court Chamber
312, 3rd Floor, M. C. Setalvad Block, In front of 'D' Gate, Bhagwan Das Road, Supreme Court of India, New Delhi 110001
Contact: 8459194576, 9811011747
www.jayprakashsomani.com

Books are available online at
1. Notion Press: https://notionpress.com/author/jayprakash_somani
2. Amazon: https://www.amazon.in/s?k=jayprakash+somani
3. Flipkart: https://www.flipkart.com/search?q=Jayprakash%20Somani

I

Indian Bank and Ors. Vs. Mahaveer Khariwal, 2021

Hon'ble Judges/Coram:
Ashok Bhushan, R. Subhash Reddy and M.R. Shah, JJ.

Equivalent Citation: 2021(1)ALT117, 2021 1 AWC496SC, 2021(I)CLR531, [2021(168)FLR853], 2021(1)J.L.J.R.382, 2021(1)PLJR402, (2021)2SCC632, 2021(1)SCT410(SC), 2021(1)SLJ347(SC), 2021(2)SLR1(SC), (2021)1UPLBEC281, MANU/SC/0034/2021

Relevant sections: Regulations 29 and 29(1) of Pension Regulations, 1995

Number of pages in original Judgment: 08

Case Note:

Service - Voluntary retirement - Allowing of - Regulations 29 and 29(1) of Pension Regulations, 1995 - Respondent-employee was working with Appellant bank-employer - Employee applied for leave as his son was admitted in hospital - Thereafter, employee wrote to the employer seeking extension of leave - Application for leave as well as the application for extension of leave were refused by employer - Employee submitted application seeking voluntary retirement from services of employer - Employer rejected request of employee for voluntary retirement on ground that employee was not eligible under Pension Regulations, 1995 - Being aggrieved by rejection of application for voluntary retirement, employee preferred Writ Petition - Single Judge dismissed writ petition so far as challenge to rejection of his voluntary retirement application - Feeling aggrieved and dissatisfied with judgment and order passed by Single Judge, e employee preferred Letters Patent Appeal before Division Bench of High Court - Division Bench had allowed appeal and had directed employer to release retiral dues of employee - Hence, present appeal - Whether rejection of request of employee for voluntary retirement was legal and in consonance with Regulation 29 of Pension Regulations, 1995.

Brief Facts:

The Respondent-employee was working with the Appellant bank-employer. The employee applied for leave as his son was admitted in the hospital. Thereafter, the employee wrote to the employer seeking extension of leave. The application for leave as well as the application for extension of leave were refused by the employer and the employee was directed to report on duty. The employee submitted an application seeking voluntary retirement from the services of the employer in accordance with Circular and the format given by the employer for submitting the notice of voluntary retirement. In the application for voluntary retirement, the employee requested for waiver of three months' notice, as required Under Regulation 29 of the Indian Bank Employees Pension Regulations, 1995 and requested/ authorised the employer to deduct the salary of the notice period from out of the amount payable by the employer on retirement. The employer rejected the request of the employee for voluntary retirement on the ground that the employee was not eligible under Pension Regulations, 1995. Being aggrieved by the rejection of the application for voluntary retirement, the employee preferred Writ Petition. The Single Judge dismissed the writ petition so far as challenge to the rejection of his voluntary retirement application vide communication. Feeling aggrieved and dissatisfied with the judgment and order passed by the Single Judge in dismissing the writ petition with respect to his prayer to quash the letter rejecting his request for voluntary retirement, the employee preferred Letters Patent Appeal before the Division Bench of the High Court. The Division Bench, by the impugned judgment and order, had allowed the said Letters Patent Appeal and had quashed and set aside the letter and had directed the employer to release retiral dues of the employee in accordance with Pension Regulations, 1995.

Held, while dismissing the appeal:

i. On a fair reading of Regulation 29, it emerges that an employee is entitled to apply for voluntary retirement after he has completed twenty years of qualifying service. He can apply for voluntary retirement by giving notice of not less than three months in writing to the appointing authority (Regulation 29(1)). However, as per proviso to Sub-regulation (1) of Regulation 29, Sub-regulation (1) of Regulation 29 shall not apply to an employee who is on deputation or on study leave on abroad unless after having been transferred or having returned to India he has resumed charge of the post in India and has served for a period of not less than one year. It also appears that as per Sub-regulation (2) of Regulation 29, the notice of voluntary retirement given under Sub-regulation (1) shall require acceptance by the appointing authority. However, as per the proviso to Sub-regulation (2), the appointing authority has to take a decision before the expiry of the period specified in the notice. It provides that where the appointing authority does not refuse to grant the permission for retirement before the expiry of the period specified in the notice, there shall be deemed acceptance of the voluntary retirement application and the retirement shall become effective from the date of expiry of the period mentioned in the notice. However, at the same time, as per Sub-regulation 3(a), an employee may make a request in writing to the appointing authority for waiver of the three months' notice and may make a request to accept the notice of voluntary retirement of less than three months giving reasons thereof. Sub-regulation 3(b) provides that on receipt of a request for waiver of three months' notice as per Sub-regulation 3(a), the appointing authority may, subject to the provisions of Sub-regulation (2), consider such request for the curtailment of the period of notice of three months on merits and if it is satisfied that the curtailment of the period of notice will not cause any administrative inconvenience, the appointing authority may relax the requirement of notice of three months on the condition that the employee shall not apply for commutation of a part of the pension before the expiry of the notice of three months. In the present case, the application of the employee submitting the voluntary retirement application with a request for curtailment of notice of three months was absolutely in consonance with Regulation 29. The request made by the employee for curtailment of the period of notice of three months was required to be considered by the appointing authority on merits and only in a case where it is found that the curtailment of the period of notice may cause any administrative inconvenience, the request for curtailment of the period of three months' notice can be rejected. On considering the communication rejecting the application of the employee for voluntary retirement, it does not reflect any compliance of Sub-regulation 3(b) of Regulation 29. As such, no reasons whatsoever had been assigned/given except stating that the request is not in accordance with Pension Regulations, 1995. Even otherwise, it was required to be noted that even the communication was on the last day of the third month, i.e., ninety day from the date of submitting the voluntary retirement application. Therefore, there was no reason to reject the prayer of curtailment of the period of notice considering the grounds mention in Sub-regulation 3(b) of Regulation 29. Be that as it may, the rejection of the application for voluntary retirement was not on the ground that notice of three months is not given. The request made by the employee for curtailment of notice of three months was also not considered on merits. Therefore, as rightly held by the Division Bench of the High Court, the application for voluntary retirement was absolutely in consonance with Regulation 29 and that the rejection was bad in law and contrary to Regulation 29. The Division Bench of the High Court was absolutely justified in quashing and setting aside the communication.

ii. So far as the submission on behalf of the employer that the employee was not eligible for voluntary retirement in view of proviso to Sub-regulation (1) of Regulation 29 as after he returned to India from another Branch he did not serve for a period of not less than one year was concerned, there was a specific finding given by the Division Bench that the said proviso shall not be applicable to the facts of the case on hand as in the present case the employee was on transfer to Colombo Branch and was not on deputation. It could not be said that the employee was sent on deputation as Chief Manager, Colombo Branch. It says that he was posted as Chief Manager of Branch. Even when he was relieved from Branch to join at another Branch in the communication, it speaks about the transfer order. It was not the order of repatriation. Therefore, proviso to Sub-regulation (1) to Regulation 29 shall not be applicable.

II

New Victoria Mills and Ors. Vs. Shrikant Arya, 2021

Hon'ble Judges/Coram:

Sanjay Kishan Kaul and M.M. Sundresh, JJ.

Equivalent Citation: AIR2021SC4635, 2021(4)SCT181(SC), MANU/SC/0709/2021

Relevant sections: Industrial Companies (Special Provisions) Act, 1985

Number of pages in original Judgment: 11

Case Note:

Service -Voluntary Retirement Scheme - Availed by tendering resignation - Subsequently cut-off date concerned extended - Resignation tendered stated by Respondent to be withdrawn - Appellant dispute the averment - High Court held in favour of the Respondent - Hence, the present appeal - Appellant contended that Respondent did not challenge letters tendering resignation - Whether Respondent's resignation in such circumstances could be held validly withdrawn?

Brief Facts:

Respondent was working as a Supervisor (Maintenance) in Appellant No. 1. The textile industry went through difficult times during the period relevant.A Modified Voluntary Retirement Scheme (MVRS/Scheme) was propounded by Appellant No. 3 to facilitate the voluntary retirement of employees. Respondent applied to avail the scheme. Resignation was tendered. General acceptance notice featuring name of Respondent issued. Notice notifying new cut-off date was issued. Respondent was asked to attend duties. Respondent addressed a letter that his resignation would be deemed as cancelled. It was contended that postponement of cut-off date would not take away the validity of acceptance of resignation. High Court's single Judge bench decided in favour of the Respondent. Division bench upheld the order. Hence, the present appeal.

Held, while allowing the Appeal:

i. The wordings of the Scheme are clear that acceptance of resignation has to simultaneously happen with the abolition of the post and thereafter, the payments have to be disbursed.
ii. Mere delay in relieving the Respondent from duties would not impact the acceptance of his resignation.
iii. The resignation letter of the Respondent stood accepted on 28.05.2003 and the Respondent is entitled to the benefits under the Scheme which have already been paid to the Respondent albeit without prejudice to the rights and contentions of the Respondent in the proceedings.
iv. The impugned order is set aside. The appeal is accordingly allowed leaving the parties to bear their own costs.

III

Union of India (UOI) and Ors. Vs. Abhiram Verma, 2021

Hon'ble Judges/Coram:
M.R. Shah and A.S. Bopanna, JJ.

Equivalent Citation: (2021)8MLJ161, 2021(II)OLR952, 2021(4)SCT223(SC), MANU/SC/0749/2021

Relevant sections: Regulation 15 of the Pension Regulations, 1961

Number of pages in original Judgment: 09

Case Note:

Service - Terminal/ Pensionary Benefits - Denial thereof - Regulation 15 of the Pension Regulations - Armed Forces Tribunal directed Appellants vide impugned judgment to process pensionary benefits by taking qualifying service as 15 years as a "late entrant" - Whether Respondent entitled to the benefit of Regulation 15 of Pension Regulations, 1961 as a "late entrant" and therefore entitled to the pensionary benefits? - Whether the resignation tendered can be said to be a "resignation" or "voluntary retirement"?

Brief Facts:

Respondent herein commissioned in the Indian Army (Armed Medical Corps) as a Short Service Commission Officer for a period of five years. He voluntarily applied for Permanent Commission and was granted. Respondent became a Graded Specialist and thereafter a Classified Specialist. Respondent applied for resignation on the ground of lack of promotional prospects which however was rejected. Thereafter Respondent filed a statutory complaint against the rejection of his resignation and the same was rejected. Writ challenging rejection was allowed by the High Court. Thereafter the Respondent's resignation was accepted, however, it was stated that he was not entitled to any terminal benefits except for encashment of leave (the denial of the terminal benefits was the subject matter before the Armed Forces Tribunal). The name of the Respondent was struck off from the Army Medical Corps vide relevant movement order. By the impugned judgment challenging above denial, the Armed Forces Tribunal directed Appellants to process the Respondent's claim for terminal/pensionary benefits taking qualifying service as 15 years as a "late entrant" under Regulation 15 of the Pension Regulations. Hence, the present appeal.

Held, while dismissing the Appeal:

i. There is a distinction between the "resignation" and "voluntary retirement". A person can resign at any time during his service, however, an officer cannot ask for premature/voluntary retirement unless he fulfills the eligibility criteria.
ii. When the legislature, in its wisdom, brings forth certain beneficial provisions in the form of Pension Regulations from a particular date and on particular terms and conditions, aspects which are excluded cannot be included in it by implication. Therefore, having tendered the "resignation", the Respondent has to suffer the consequences and now cannot be permitted to take 'U' turn and say that what the Respondent wanted was "premature retirement" and not "resignation".
iii. As per Regulation 15, a "late entrant" is an officer who is retired on reaching the prescribed age limit for compulsory retirement with at least 15 years commissioned service (actual). As the Respondent did not retire on reaching the prescribed age limit for compulsory retirement, the Respondent cannot be said to be a "late entrant". Respondent therefore not entitled to the benefit of Regulation 15 and therefore not entitled to the pensionary benefits.
iv. Impugned judgment and order quashed and set aside. Respondent is not entitled to the terminal/pensionary benefits as a "late entrant" in terms of Regulation 15 of the Pension. Regulations. Appeal allowed accordingly.

IV

Rajasthan State Road Transport Corporation Ltd. and Ors. Vs. Mohani Devi and Ors., 2020

Hon'ble Judges/Coram:

R. Banumathi and A.S. Bopanna, JJ.

Equivalent Citation: AIR2020SC2118, 2021(3)BLJ441, 2020(II)CLR205, 2020(2)ESC398(SC), [2020(166)FLR386], (2020)IILLJ565SC, (2020)5SCC741, (2020)2SCC(LS)239, 2020 (6) SCJ 246, 2020(2)SCT632(SC), 2020(3)SLJ36(SC), 2020(3)SLR98(SC), MANU/SC/0373/2020

Relevant sections: Rule 50 of Rajasthan Civil Services Pension Rules, 1996

Number of pages in original Judgment: 05

Case Note:

Service - Resignation - Retiral benefits - In course of service, Respondent's husband had moved application seeking voluntary retirement from service in which no order was passed - Subsequently, Respondent's husband submitted his resignation which was accepted - Thereafter, Respondent's husband submitted application mentioned that no decision had been taken by authorities on his first application and therefore he should be treated as having voluntarily retired with consequent retiral benefits - Respondent after her husband's death approached High Court - Single Judge directed Appellants to treat Respondent's husband as having voluntarily retired and release retiral benefits to which he was entitled - Aggrieved, appeal was filed by Appellants before Division Bench - Division Bench found no infirmity in reasoning of Single Judge - Hence, present appeal - Whether High Court was justified in arriving at conclusion that resignation submitted by husband of Respondent be considered as application for voluntary retirement and treat cessation of jural relationship of employer/employee under provision for Voluntary Retirement.

Brief Facts:

In the course of service, Respondent's husband had moved an application seeking voluntary retirement from service indicating health reasons. No order was passed on the said application for voluntary retirement and the Respondent's husband continued to remain in service. Subsequently, the Respondent's husband submitted his resignation as he claimed to be under depression and his health condition had further deteriorated. The resignation was accepted by the authorities, he was relieved of his duties and the benefits were paid. Thereafter, the Respondent's husband was stated to have immediately submitted an application pointing out that he had erred in mentioning resignation and he desired to retire in view of his earlier application for voluntary retirement. The application also mentioned that no decision had been taken by authorities on his first application and therefore he should be treated as having voluntarily retired with consequent retiral benefits. The Respondent after her husband's death approached the High Court with such prayer. The Single Judge held that the Respondent's husband had moved an application indicating deteriorating health and forcing such employee to work would be an act of oppression. Additionally, it was held that the voluntary retirement application was not decided within the period prescribed as per the Clause 19-D(2) of the Pension Scheme and reliance was placed on Clause 18-D(2) of RSRTC Standing Orders as per which an employee of the Corporation who had rendered pensionable service was entitled to seek voluntary retirement. It held that the Respondent's husband would be deemed to have retired even though he had moved another application terming his retirement as resignation. Thus, the Appellants were directed to treat Respondent's husband as having voluntarily retired and release the retiral benefits to which he was entitled. Aggrieved, an appeal was filed by the Appellants before the Division Bench. However, no infirmity was found by the Division Bench in the reasoning of the Single Judge and the Division Bench dismissed the appeal.

Held, while allowing the appeal:

i. The factual aspects which were relevant for decision making in the instant case had not been referred by the High Court during the course of its order but has merely assumed that the voluntary retirement application should be deemed to have been accepted when there was no rejection. As noticed from the objection statement filed by the Respondent herein herself, the right to seek for voluntary retirement was stipulated in Rule 50 of Rajasthan Civil Services Pension Rules, 1996. Since the same provides for twenty years of qualifying service, the Respondent's husband had qualified to apply. However, what was relevant to take note was that Sub-rule (2) thereof provides that the notice of voluntary retirement given by the employee shall require acceptance by the appointing authority. In the instant case, the undisputed position is that there was no acceptance and in that circumstance the husband of the Respondent had submitted his resignation. Though the High Court has indicated deemed acceptance, the same would not be justified in the instant facts since the position which had not been taken note by the High Court was that as on the date when the husband of the Respondent had made the application for voluntary retirement the husband of the Respondent had already been issued Charge-Sheets alleging misconduct. Though the Respondent, through the objection statement seeks to contend that the charge alleged against her husband was not justified, that aspect of the matter would not be germane to the present consideration. Hence there would be no obligation to accept. In the instant facts the proceedings relating to the charge sheet was taken forward and completed through the final order. The punishment of withholding of the increment was imposed. In such circumstance the non-consideration of the application for voluntary retirement would be justified.

The inquiry had been completed and thereafter when the Respondent's husband submitted the resignation, the same was processed, accepted, he was relieved and the payment of terminal benefits were made which had been accepted by him. During his lifetime, the husband did not raise any issue with regard to the same. It was only thereafter the Respondent has filed the writ petition before the High Court. Primarily it was to be noticed that when the application for voluntary retirement was filed and had not been favourably considered by the employer, instead of submitting the resignation, if any legal right was available the appropriate course ought to have been to seek for acceptance of the application by initiating appropriate legal proceedings. Instead the Respondent's husband had yielded to the position of non-acceptance of the application for voluntary retirement and had thereafter submitted his resignation. The acceptance of the resignation was acted upon by receiving the terminal benefits. If that be the position, when the writ petition was filed belatedly and that too after the death of the employee who had not raised any grievance during his life time, consideration of the prayer made by the Respondent was not justified. The High Court had, therefore, committed an error in passing the concurrent orders.

V

Assistant General Manager and Ors. Vs. Radhey Shyam Pandey, 2020

Hon'ble Judges/Coram:

Arun Mishra, M.R. Shah and B.R. Gavai, JJ.

Equivalent Citation: 2020(8)ADJ179, 2020 6 AWC5782SC, 2021(1)BLJ73, 2020(II)CLR51, 2021(1)ESC299(SC), (2020)6SCC438, (2020)2SCC(LS)523, 2020 (5) SCJ 347, 2020(2)SCT305(SC), 2020(5)SLR282(SC), MANU/SC/0252/2020

Relevant sections: Rule 22(i)(a) of Pension Fund Rules; Articles 14, 15, 16 and 21 of Constitution of India

Number of pages in original Judgment: 40

Case Note:

Service - Pension - Voluntarily retirement scheme - After obtaining approval of Government of India, Indian Bank Association (IBA) evolved Voluntary Retirement Scheme (VRS) - Central Board of Directors of Bank adopted and approved scheme in its meeting for implementing VRS for employees of bank by retiring them on completion of fifteen years of service with benefit provided in scheme - After Central Board of SBI approved proposals, circular was issued which made it clear that gratuity, provident fund contribution as per the Provident Fund Rules, pension in terms of SBI Employees' Pension Fund Rules, leave encashment to be provided beside amount of ex gratia- Respondent questioned refusal of bank to pay pension in writ application filed in High Court - Respondent retired and bank accepted offer of employee to retire him voluntarily - High Court held that case of employee fell under Second Part of Rule 22(i)(a) of Rules and admissible benefit could not be denied - Hence, present appeal - Whether Respondent-employees were entitled to pension on completion of fifteen years of service as per State Bank of India Voluntary Retirement Scheme.

Brief Facts:

After obtaining approval of the Government of India, the Indian Bank Association (IBA) evolved a Voluntary Retirement Scheme. The Central Board of Directors of the State Bank of India (SBI) adopted and approved the scheme in its meeting for implementing the VRS for the employees of the bank by retiring them on completion of fifteen years of service with the benefit provided in the scheme. The scheme had been drawn up, keeping in view the guidelines issued by the IBA. After the Central Board of SBI approved the proposals contained in the memorandum, a circular was issued in which it was mentioned that the IBA advised that as the Committee constituted by the Finance Ministry recommended introduction of a VRS in order to rationalise the manpower, the Government of India had no objection for adopting and implementing the VRS. It was clearly stated in the Circular that the Central Board of Directors accorded approval for adopting and implementing the SBI voluntary Retirement Scheme drawn up, keeping in view the guidelines issued by the IBA. The circular also made it clear that gratuity, provident fund contribution as per the Provident Fund Rules, pension in terms of the SBI Employees' Pension Fund Rules, leave encashment to be provided beside the amount of ex gratia. Respondent questioned the refusal of the bank to pay pension in the writ application filed in the High Court. He retired under the SBI VRS. The bank accepted the offer of the employee to retire him voluntarily. He was aged fifteen years three months and had nine months service still to go before attaining the age of superannuation. When the VRS became effective, he had put in nineteen years, nine months, and eighteen days of pensionable service. He had to retire on completion of sixty years, and would have put in a little more than twenty years of pensionable service. The High Court held that the case of the employee fell under the Second Part of Rule 22(i)(a). He was in service of the bank and completed ten years of pensionable service, and further, he attained the age of fifty eight years before the date he retired. The High Court opined that the clarification was not part of the VRS scheme.

The employee retired outside Rule as per the contractual retirement scheme. The contract had to prevail. In Pension Fund Rules, Clause (a) in Rule 22(i) was inserted to give the employees the benefit of pension after ten years of pensionable service even if they had joined late. The High Court found that the matter was covered by Rule 22(i)(a). The admissible benefit could not be denied. If a contracting party is entitled to take benefit of a permissible clause, then it could not be denied to him.

Held, while disposing off the appeals:

i. The VRS scheme was not floated by the SBI on its own volition. It was pursuant to an exercise that was undertaken by the IBA in view of the recent developments of modern technology considering the age group of the employees in the bank, the need to have a new skill, and to rationalise the manpower, a decision was taken. It was decided at the Government level to provide pension after completion of fifteen years of service as a special measure, the banks were bound to implement it in that manner or not at all. The Central Board of Directors of the SBI accepted the VRS proposal of Government and IBA without any reservation of not providing pension along with other benefits, as mandated in the VRS scheme. The action of the instrumentality of the State could not be violative of Article 14. It could not be permitted to act arbitrarily. Articles 15 and 16 provide for equality and provide for an umbrella against discrimination.

ii. Though the Deputy General Manager was authorised by the Central Board of Directors to amend, modify or cancel the VRS. The Rules were amended by other banks. It was not stated in answer to the query that under the VRS scheme, a person who had rendered fifteen years of qualifying service would not be entitled to a pension. Nor it was so stated in resolution of the Central Board of SBI. That apart, Deputy General Manager tried to interpret VRS scheme in isolation without considering what was approved by the Board. Not only the scheme but also the memorandum have to be read together to understand resolution of Board. Once the memorandum containing the IBAs proposal of providing pension was approved in absolute terms, the clarification could not be of any value to dilute the otherwise clear and unambiguous resolution of the Board of Directors. The Deputy General Manager did not have any such wide and arbitrary power to defeat the claim of the employees for pension on completion of fifteen years of permanent service, which was their right. The action of D.G.M. could not be said to be in accordance with the resolution. The pension was the essence of the scheme, depriving it could not be said to be authorised, such action can only be termed as unfair and unreasonable and patently violative of Articles 14, 16, and 21 of the Constitution of India.

iii. It was apparent that once the Central Board of Directors accepted the memorandum for making payment of pension, in case it was not accepting the proposal in the memorandum, it ought to have said clearly that it was not ready to accept the proposals of the Government and the IBA and rejects the same. Once it approved the proposals referred to in the memorandum, which were on the basis of IBA's letter and Government of India's decision it was bound to implement it in true letter and spirit. By accepting the same, binding obligation was created upon the SBI to make payment of pension on completion of fifteen years of service. It could not invalidate its own decision by relying on fact it failed to amend the rule, whereas other Banks did it later on with retrospective effect. They could not invalidate otherwise valid decision by virtue of exclusive superior power to amend or not to amend the Rule and act unfairly and make the entire contract unreasonable based on misrepresentation. It was open to the Board of Directors to reject the proposal. Once it accepted the proposal to make payment of pension on completion of fifteen years of service as proposed in the memorandum, though the scheme is tried to be interpreted by the SBI that pension was to be admissible as provided in the Rule that refers to proportionate pension as noted by this Court in O.P. Swarnakar and Ors., and what was decided by Government of India/IBA, was not taken away rather adopted by the Central Board of Directors. The scheme of contractual nature had to be read in the context and in the backdrop of facts and what has been resolved by the Board of Directors. There was no ambiguity with respect to the admissibility of pension when the memorandum and the scheme are read together. In case of ambiguity and even if two interpretations are possible in the backdrop of facts of the case, one in favour of the employees has to be adopted and so-called clarification even if considered in the manner so as to deny the benefit of pension, had to be held to be unenforceable, illegal and contrary to law.

iv. It was apparent from the eligibility Clause of the VRS scheme that eligibility was provided for the employees having fifteen years of pensionable service and they would be entitled for benefits as provided in the scheme. The eligibility clause, when read with clauses providing the benefit, leaves no room for any doubt and makes it clear that employees with fifteen years of service were treated as eligible to claim the benefit of the scheme floated by SBI. It was not the provision in the VRS scheme that incumbents having completed 20 years of service would be entitled for pensionary benefits. The scheme was carved out specially for attracting the employees by providing pension and other benefits to eligible persons like ex gratia, gratuity, pension and leave encashment. Deprivation of pension would make them ineligible for the benefits and would run repugnant to the eligibility clause.

v. The employees who completed fifteen years of service or more as on cut-off date were entitled to proportionate pension under SBI VRS to be computed as per SBI Pension Fund Rules. Let the benefits be extended to all such similar employees retired under VRS on completion of fifteen years of service without requiring them to rush to the court. However, considering the facts and circumstances, it would not be appropriate to burden the bank with interest.

VI

Karan Singh Vs. Delhi Transport Corporation and Ors., 2019

Hon'ble Judges/Coram:
Mohan M. Shantanagoudar and Ajay Rastogi, JJ.

Equivalent Citation: 2020(I)CLR449, 2020(1)ESC6(SC), 2020(1)SLR114(SC), MANU/SC/2083/2019

Relevant sections: Rule 22 and Rule 3(1)(q) of Central Civil Services Pension Rules, 1972

Number of pages in original Judgment: 05

Case Note:

Service - Pension - Minimum qualifying period - Appellant offered appointment after qualifying written test for post of Conductor - Appellant since had crossed age of forty years, submitted his application for voluntary retirement which was allowed and various payments were made as per scheme but no order for pension was passed - Appellant filed original application before Central Administrative Tribunal whereby Corporation was directed to pay Appellant pension and other benefits in accordance with the pension scheme - On appeal, High Court set aside order passed by Tribunal - Whether Appellant had completed ten years of qualifying service in terms of scheme of Rules which makes him entitled for pension under pension scheme introduced by Corporation.

Brief Facts:

The Appellant offered appointment after qualifying the written test held for the post of Conductor. He was given regular appointment as monthly rate conductor. The Respondent-Corporation notified voluntary retirement scheme which states that those employees who had ten years of service in the Corporation or completed forty years of age were entitled to opt for voluntary retirement under the scheme. The Appellant since had crossed the age of forty years, submitted his application for voluntary retirement which was allowed and various payments were made as per scheme but no order for pension was passed. Appellant filed original application before Central Administrative Tribunal whereby the Corporation was directed to pay the Appellant pension and other benefits in accordance with the pension scheme introduced by the Transport Corporation. However, High Court on appeal set aside order passed by the Tribunal.

Held, while dismissing the appeal:

i. The comparative statement of the break-up of service of the Appellant rendered clearly indicates that he was appointed after qualifying the training of two months as Conductor and the period other than two months of training which he consumed as a Retainer Crew or Conductor was neither a training nor a service which he rendered in the Corporation and it was the period consumed to qualify the written test and to await order of appointment. In the facts and circumstances, even if the two months period of training in terms of Rule 22 of Central Civil Services Pension Rules, 1972 was taken note of, the qualifying service of the Appellant comes to nine years four months and six days.

ii. So far as ninety days leave without pay was concerned, this matter was earlier heard and noticing the fact that the effect of leave without pay even sanctioned be treated as a disruption in service or to be counted in qualifying service had been referred to be decided by the larger Bench in Delhi Transport Corporation v. Balwan Singh and Ors., this Court kept the matter pending awaiting the decision. Since this issue had now been decided by a three Judge Bench of this Court in which this Court taking note of Rule 3(1)(q) and Rule 21 of the scheme of Rules has held that the period of leave for which salary is payable would be taken into account for determining the pensionable service, while the period for which leave salary is not payable would be excluded.

iii. In the instant facts and circumstances and taking note of the view expressed by the three Judge Bench of this Court in Delhi Transport Corporation v. Balwan Singh and Ors., the Appellant failed to qualify with the minimum qualifying service of ten years which could make him entitled to claim pension under the pension Scheme, 1993.

VII

State of West Bengal and Ors. Vs. Tonmoy Mondal, 2019

Hon'ble Judges/Coram:

Arun Mishra, Navin Sinha and Indira Banerjee, JJ.

Equivalent Citation: 2019(5)SCALE551, (2019)16SCC348, 2019(2)SCT566(SC), 2020(1)SLR325(SC), MANU/SC/0472/2019

Relevant sections: Rule 75 of West Bengal Service Rules, 1971; Article 309 of Constitution of India, 1950

Number of pages in original Judgment: 08

Ratio Decidendi:

Merely by entertaining a different view as to interpretation of a particular provision, a judgment could not be reviewed

Case Note:

Service - Interpretation of Rule - Voluntary retirement - Entitlement - Rule 75 of West Bengal Service Rules, 1971 and Article 309 of Constitution of India, 1950 - Question involved in appeal was interpretation of Rule 75 of Rules, 1971 framed in exercise of powers conferred by proviso to Article 309 of Constitution - Whether submission of Appellant that, it was not proper for Division Bench to review previous judgment and order as no ground within parameters of review jurisdiction was available was liable to be accepted. Facts: Respondent-Dr. Tonmoy Mondal had joined services as a Medical Officer in West Bengal Health Services on ad hoc basis. He was confirmed in said post vide Notification dated 15th November, 2002. Respondent sought voluntary retirement. Prayer made by Respondent was rejected by Government vide order on ground that, it was not considered appropriate in public interest to accept request for voluntary retirement. Respondent questioned order by way of filing Original Application before Tribunal. Tribunal vide order allowed application and quashed order passed by State government declining voluntary retirement. State of West Bengal filed Writ Petition in High Court challenging the same. Division Bench of High Court initially vide judgment opined that, according to Note 3 below Rule 75(aaa) of Rules, every case of retirement under Rule 75 was to be examined by appointing authority on facts of case concerned. Permission granted to one Medical Officer to retire under Rule could not necessarily lead to conclusion that, another Medical Officer seeking to retire under Rule was also entitled to permission. Extent of public interest involved in case was to be examined by appointing authority objectively and opinion formed by appointing authority as to existence of public interest could not be judicially reviewed unless it was case that, it was recorded with malice or ex facie without any basis. While setting aside order of Tribunal, High Court upheld order passed by State Government declining to accept prayer for voluntary retirement. Petition was preferred in present Court against decision rendered by High Court. However, it was withdrawn on ground of certain errors apparent on face of record. Thereafter, Petitioner wanted to file a review petition. Permission was granted to withdraw Special Leave Petition with liberty to file a review petition. Division Bench while allowing review petition had observed that, on a proper interpretation, Note 3 of Rule 75 could not have been rationally or logically applied in respect of Sub-rule (aaa) of Rule 75 of the Rules. There was an error apparent on face of record in judgment dated 22nd August, 2014 as such, same was required to be interfered with.

Held, while allowing the appeal:

i. Merely on entertaining a different view on the interpretation of Rule 75, it was not open to Division Bench to review previous judgment and order passed by a different Division Bench of High Court on 22nd August, 2014. A fundamental jurisdictional error had been committed by Division Bench of High Court while setting aside order. It had acted as if it was exercising appellate power while exercising the review jurisdiction. There was no such error apparent on face of the record in previous judgment warranting review by the different bench of High Court. Merely by entertaining a different view as to interpretation of a particular provision, a judgment could not be reviewed.

ii. Yet another jurisdictional error had been committed. Once Court had found that, there was sufficient reason for reviewing order, only review petition should have been decided, after recall of order, it ought to have heard main matter afresh. That had not been done. By the same impugned order, the previous judgment and order have been set aside and main case had also been disposed of without hearing it again separately. Thus, proper procedure had not been followed.

iii. Rule 75(a) dealt with retirement on attaining age of superannuation. Expression "compulsory" retirement had been wrongly used in said provision. No one to continue in service after attaining age of 58 years, as per definition of compulsory retirement. Retirement on attaining age of superannuation was not a concept of compulsory retirement as understood in service jurisprudence. State might be well advised to amend rule.

iv. Rule 75 (aa) dealt with retirement in public interest. As a matter of fact, concept of compulsory retirement was one which was to be found in Rule 75 (aa). It provided that, there was an absolute right with State Government in public interest to retire a person by giving a notice of not less than 3 months in writing or 3 months' pay and allowances in lieu of such notice.

v. As per, Rule 75 (aaa) of Rules, it was apparent that, same dealt with voluntary retirement of a government employee. Any Government employee by giving notice of not less than 3 months in writing or 3 months' pay and allowances in lieu of such notice, to appointing authority, might retire from government service after he had attained age of 50 years, if he was in Group A or Group B (erstwhile gazette) service or post and had entered Government service before attaining the age of 35 years, and in all other cases, after he had attained age of 55 years, provided that it shall be open to appointing authority to withhold permission to a government employee under suspension who seeks to retire under this sub-rule.

vi. Note 1 to Rule 75 (aaa) provided that, in computing three months notice period referred to in Rule 75 (a) and (aaa) date of service of notice and date of expiry shall be excluded.

vii. Note 2 specifically dealt with three months notice referred in Rule (aa) and Sub-rule (aaa) that, it might be given before government employee attained age specified in said sub-rules provided that, retirement took place after Government employee has attained specified age.

viii. Note 3 was not confined in operation to Sub-rule (aaa) of Rule 75. It was clearly provided in Note 3 that, appointing authority should invariably keep on record that, in his opinion, it was necessary to retire Government employee in pursuance of aforesaid Rule in public interest. Note 3 was applicable to both Rule 75 (aa) and 75 (aaa) as was rightly opined by Division Bench while rendering judgment.

ix. In previous judgment and order passed by Division Bench on 22.08.2014 had taken a correct view on merits and was illegally interfered with while exceeding jurisdiction by subsequent Division Bench while reviewing it and dismissing Writ Petition.

x. Respondent was directed to report back to duty within one month. He would not be entitled to wages for period he had not served and that would also not be counted towards period of service for purpose of retiral benefits.

xi. Impugned order was set aside. Appeal allowed.

VIII

Central Bank of India and Ors. Vs. Tara Chand, 2019

Hon'ble Judges/Coram:

Ashok Bhushan and Navin Sinha, JJ.

Equivalent Citation: AIR2019SC4344, 2019(III)CLR1, 2019(3)ESC692(SC), [2019(163)FLR626], 2019LabIC4561, (2019)6MLJ436, 2019(10)SCALE231, 2019(4)SCT21(SC), 2019(3)SLJ1(SC), 2019(6)SLR773(SC), (2019)4UPLBEC3042, MANU/SC/1014/2019

Relevant sections: Regulations 14 and 28 of Central Bank of India (Employees') Pension Regulations, 1995; Clause 6(ii) of Central Bank of India Employees Voluntary Retirement Scheme, 2001.

Number of pages in original Judgment: 08

Case Note:

Service - Pensionary benefits - Regulations 14 and 28 of Central Bank of India (Employees') Pension Regulations, 1995 - Present appeal had been filed by Central Bank of India challenging judgment of Division Bench of High Court dismissing Special Appeal filed by Appellants and quashing order of Bank denying to grant pro-rata pension upon opting for voluntary retirement under Central Bank of India Employees Voluntary Retirement Scheme, 2001 - Whether Respondent was rightly held entitled to pension under Clause 6(ii) of Scheme, 2001.

Brief Facts:

On 26th October, 1995, Regulations, 1995 came into force. The Respondent-Tara Chand opted for the pension scheme. The Respondent's option for pension scheme was accepted by the Bank. A Scheme for voluntary retirement, namely, Central Bank of India Employees Voluntary Retirement Scheme, 2001(Scheme, 2001) was framed. Prior to the Scheme being made effective a circular dated 31.01.2001 was issued by the Bank by which several clarifications were issued for smooth implementation of the Scheme. The Respondent submitted an application for voluntary retirement. The application for voluntary retirement of Respondent was accepted by the Bank. By order, the Bank refused to grant pro-rata pension to the Respondent No. 1, who had opted for the voluntary retirement under the Scheme, 2001. Writ Petition was filed by the Respondent. The learned Single Judge after considering the Regulations, 1995 and the Scheme, 2001 took the view that Clause 6(ii) of the Scheme, 2001 entitled the Respondent to pension as per Pension Regulations, 1995. The writ petition was allowed and the order was set aside with direction to the Bank to extend benefits of pro-rata/proportionate pension to the Respondent to the extent of his entitlement in terms of the Scheme, 2001 read with Regulations, 1995. The Bank aggrieved by the judgment of the learned Single Judge filed Special Appeal, which too had been dismissed by the Division Bench. The Division Bench took the view that the Respondent who was above 40 years of age and had completed 11 years of service in the Bank was definitely entitled to opt for voluntary retirement and simultaneously claim pension under the Scheme. The Division Bench took the view that Clause 6(ii) of the Scheme, 2001 entitles the Respondent to pension.

Held, while allowing the appeal:

i. It is true that, as per Clause 4, any employee who has 15 years of service or completed 40 years of age is eligible to apply for voluntary retirement under the Scheme. There is no dispute that the Respondent was eligible to apply for voluntary retirement, other benefits under the Scheme have been extended to the Respondent and only limited issue in the present appeal is entitlement of the Respondent for pension. Payment of pension under the Scheme has to be as per Pension Regulations, 1995.
ii. Regulation 14 begins with the words subject to the other conditions contained in these regulations. Further, an employee who has rendered a minimum of ten years of service in the Bank on the date of his retirement or the date on which he is deemed to have retired shall qualify for

pension. Thus, this qualifying service is relevant when a person has completed 10 years of service on the date of his retirement.

iii. Voluntary retirement in the case of Respondent is not retirement which is covered within the definition of Clause 2(y) on strict interpretation of definition clause. Furthermore, said qualifying service is subject to the other conditions contained in Regulations. Chapter V of the Regulations, 1995 deals with classes of pension. Different classes of pension include superannuation pension, pension on voluntary retirement, invalid pension, compassionate allowance, premature retirement pension and compulsory retirement pension. Classes of pension specifically defined in Chapter V and in a sense retirement under Voluntary Retirement Scheme was not contemplated when the Regulations were made in 1995. Regulation 28 was amended in the year 2002 w.e.f. 01.09.2000 whereby an employee who opts for retirement before superannuation, but after rendering service for a minimum period of 15 years was also entitled for pension. The Respondent is not covered by proviso to Regulation 28. As per Clause 6(ii) of the Scheme 2001 entitlement being on the basis of Pension Regulations, 1995, the Respondent shall be entitled only for pension if he falls in any of the classes of pension in Chapter V. Proviso to Regulation 28 although was amended w.e.f. 01.09.2000 but it was clarified by Circular dated 31.01.2001 that the employees, who opted for pension but completed minimum 15 years of service and opt for voluntary retirement under this Scheme would also be eligible for pro-rata pension.

iv. High Court has not correctly interpreted the Scheme and the Regulations. On the submission of the learned Counsel for the Respondent in the facts of the present case that this Court may not interfere with the impugned judgment since the Respondent is waiting for the last 18 years to receive pension, present Court is of the view that when the Court has to examine interpretation of a statutory Regulation, Scheme and the benefits to be extended to the employees, statutory regime in the Scheme has to be adhered to and with regard to the case of one individual, no exception can be made.

v. Judgments of the High Court are set aside. Appeal allowed.

ꕤ

IX

State of Uttar Pradesh and Ors. Vs. Achal Singh, 2018

Hon'ble Judges/Coram:

Arun Mishra and S. Abdul Nazeer, JJ.

Equivalent Citation: AIR2018SC3940, 2018(6) ALJ 614, 2019 (134) ALR 365, 2018(3)ESC459(SC), 2018(4)J.L.J.R.2, 2018LabIC3981, 2018(4)PLJR40, 2018(10)SCALE89, (2019)1SCC(LS)677, 2019 (1) SCJ 223, 2018(4)SCT59(SC), 2018(3)SLJ360(SC), 2018(5)SLR619(SC), MANU/SC/0879/2018

Relevant sections: Rule56 of Uttar Pradesh Fundamental Rules

Number of pages in original Judgment: 19

Case Note:

Service - Voluntary retirement - Denial of - Rule 56 of Uttar Pradesh Fundamental Rules - Respondent was working as Joint Director in Medical, Health and Family Welfare, filed application for voluntary retirement - Applications remained unattended and no order had been communicated, hence writ petitions were filed in High Court - High Court allowed writ petitions seeking voluntary retirement from Government services - Hence, present appeal - Whether under Rule 56 of Rules as amended, an employee had unfettered right to seek voluntary retirement by serving notice of three months to State Government.

Brief Facts:

Respondent was working as Joint Director in Medical, Health and Family Welfare, filed an application for voluntary retirement. The applications remained unattended and no order had been communicated, hence writ petitions were filed in the High Court. The High Court allowed writ petitions filed by the Respondents seeking voluntary retirement from the Government services.

Held, while allowing the appeal:

i. The concept of public interest could also be invoked by the Government when voluntary retirement sought by an employee, would be against the public interest. The provisions cannot be said to be violative of any of the rights. There was already paucity of the doctors as observed by the High Court, the system could not be left without competent senior persons and particularly, the High Court had itself observed that doctors are not being attracted to join services and there was an existing scarcity of the doctors. Poorest of the poor obtain treatment at the Government hospitals. They could not be put at the peril, even when certain doctors are posted against the administrative posts. It was not that they have been posted against their seniority or to the other cadre. Somebody had to man these administrative posts also, which were absolutely necessary to run the medical services which are part and parcel of the right to life itself. In the instant case, where the right of the public were involved in obtaining treatment, the State Government had taken a decision as per Explanations to decline the prayer for voluntary retirement considering the public interest. It could not be said that State had committed any illegality or its decision suffers from any vice of arbitrariness.
ii. The action of the State Government was appropriate in disallowing the prayer seeking voluntary retirement. The Government may fill the vacancies if any. But that would not bring doctors of experience at senior level and exodus of doctors could not be permitted to weaken the services when the public interest requires to serve for the sake of efficient medical profession and fulfil Directive Principles of State Policy once they found statutory expression in the Rules could not be made mockery. When services were required, denial of voluntary retirement was permissible under the Rules applicable in the State of Uttar Pradesh.
iii. Therefore, the impugned judgment and order passed by the High Court stand set aside.

ഇ

X

State Bank of Patiala and Ors. Vs. Kanwal Nain Singh, 2018

Hon'ble Judges/Coram:

Kurian Joseph, Mohan M. Shantanagoudar and Navin Sinha, JJ.

Equivalent Citation: 2018(III)CLR835, [2018(157)FLR860], 2018(3)LLN560(SC), (2018)4MLJ254, 2018(5)SCALE728, (2019)1SCC(LS)405, 2018(2)SCT505(SC), 2018(3)SLR799(SC), MANU/SC/0388/2018

Relevant sections:

Number of pages in original Judgment: 03

Case Note:

Service - Voluntary retirement - Validity thereof - Respondent filed petition virtually seeking to resurrect judgment which he suffered at hands of Court, against which even review at instance of Respondent was dismissed - Division Bench of High Court allowed same - Hence present appeal by Appellant - Whether order allowing withdrawal of application of voluntary retirement filed by Respondent was maintainable

Brief Facts:

Respondent filed application for clarification praying for enhanced ex-gratia, on basis of length of service actually rendered and scale of pay in promoted post. That application was withdrawn without prejudice to liberty to pursue any alternative remedy, if any, available in accordance with law.

Respondent filed fresh petition before High Court, virtually seeking to resurrect judgment which he suffered at hands of Court, against which even review at instance of Respondent was dismissed. Division Bench of High Court allowed the same. Hence present appeal was filed by Appellant.

Held, while allowing the appeal:

Respondent had suffered judgment when Court allowed appeal filed by Appellant and dismissed application filed by Respondent. The High Court, with great respect, was not correct in its approach in reopening case of Respondent on basis of subsequent judgment of Court in Food Corporation of India and Ors. v. Ramesh Kumar in the matter of withdrawal of application for voluntary retirement before same was accepted. As far as Respondent was concerned, his fate was sealed when Court declared that he was bound by provision in Scheme that application once made was irrevocable. For all intents and purposes, Respondent was bound by that judgment for ever. Impugned order of High Court was set aside.

XI

National Insurance Special Voluntary Retired/Retired Employees Association and Ors. Vs. United India Insurance Co. Ltd. and Ors., 2018

Hon'ble Judges/Coram:

Kurian Joseph and Sanjay Kishan Kaul, JJ.

Equivalent Citation: AIR2018SC5476, 2019 1 AWC108SC, 2019(I)CLR22, 2019(1)ESC21(SC), [2019(161)FLR241], 2018(4)J.L.J.R.339, 2018(3)JLJ646, 2019LabIC427, 2018(4)PLJR343, 2018(14)SCALE318, (2019)2SCC(LS)219, 2018(4)SCT770(SC), 2019(1)SLR364(SC), MANU/SC/1214/2018

Relevant sections: Section 17-A of the General Insurance Business (Nationalisation) Act, 1972

Number of pages in original Judgment: 07

Case Note:

Service - Benefit of scheme - Entitlement - Section 17-A of the General Insurance Business (Nationalisation) Act, 1972 - Appeal was against order denying benefit for under the scheme - Question for consideration was whether beneficiaries under SVRS-2004 Scheme, which specifically excluded benefit of additional five years' service of 1995 Scheme, would still be entitled to claim said amount contrary to explicit terms.

Brief Facts:

Appellants were ex-employees of Respondent Insurance Companies, who initially joined as Assistants, between 1972 to 1980, and went out of service taking advantage of General Insurance Employees' Special Voluntary Retirement Scheme, 2004 ('SVRS-2004 Scheme'). Bone of contention was plea of these Appellants, that they were also entitled to certain benefits arising under earlier scheme known as The General Insurance (Employees) Pension Scheme, 1995 ('1995 Scheme'), which provided that, qualifying service of an employee, retiring under that 1995 Scheme, would be increased by a period not exceeding five (5) years, subject to certain conditions. Learned Single Judge opined that, since Clause 6(1)(c) of SVRS-2004 Scheme did not specifically exclude benefits under para 30(5) of 1995 Scheme, there was no reason to deny same to beneficiaries of SVRS-2004 Scheme. Aforesaid judgment was assailed before the learned Division Bench, which, however, opined to contrary and dismissed original writ petition vide judgment. It was this judgment which had been assailed.

Held, while dismissing the appeals:

SVRS-2004 Scheme was statutory in character, being a Scheme under Section 17-A of Act, 1972. It would not be appropriate to add or subtract terms from Scheme, which had a statutory flavour. There could not have been any concession contrary to terms of Scheme, and if such a concession was to enure for benefit of retirees, then it had to go through process of a formal notification. Statutory or contractual, such voluntary retirement schemes as SVRS-2004 Scheme had to be strictly adhered to, and very objective of having such Schemes would be defeated, if parts of other Schemes were sought to be imported into such voluntary retirement schemes. What was offered by employer was a package as contained in Schemes of voluntary retirement, and that alone would be admissible. It was, thus, abundantly clear that, nothing more would be given than what was stated in Scheme, and for that matter, nothing less. If employees availed of benefit of such a Scheme with their eyes open, they could not look here and there, under different schemes, to see what other benefits could be achieved by them, by seeking to take advantage of more beneficial schemes, while simultaneously enjoying more beneficial aspects of SVRS-2004 Scheme. There was no reason to interfere with the impugned order. Appeals dismissed

XII

Surjeet Singh Bhamra Vs. Bank of India and Ors., 2016

Hon'ble Judges/Coram:

Jasti Chelameswar and Abhay Manohar Sapre, JJ.

Equivalent Citation: AIR2016SC782, 2016(2)AJR403, 2016(3)ALLMR403, 2016 2 AWC2113SC, 2016(I)CLR647, 2016(1)ESC127(SC), [2016(149)FLR1088], 2016(2)J.L.J.R.301, 2016(1)JLJ241, 2016LabIC1201, 2016(3)LLN273(SC), 2016(2)LLN12(SC), (2016)1MLJ868, 2016(2)SCALE233, (2016)4SCC204, (2016)1SCC(LS)608, 2016 (3) SCJ 389, 2016(1)SCT770(SC), 2016(3)SLJ1(SC), 2016(3)SLR22(SC), MANU/SC/0141/2016

Relevant sections: Clause 4(f) of Bank of India Officer Employees' Regulations, 1976

Number of pages in original Judgment: 10

Case Note:

Service - Voluntary retirement scheme - Application thereof - Appellant applied for voluntary retirement - Meanwhile, Appellant found guilty of irregularities - Penalty of reduction of pay imposed - Appellant's application for voluntary retirement also got approved - Appellant challenged penalty - Appellant alleged application for voluntary retirement delayed in view of scheme - Appellant was deemed retired before penal action - No employer-employee relation present, thus, penalty not legally justified - Appellant failed in all proceedings upto High Court - Hence, present Appeal - Whether the Scheme in question is mandatory or directory for ensuring their compliance by Appellant and Bank - Whether Scheme provided deemed fiction - Whether penal action was justified

Brief Facts:

This appeal is filed against the final judgment and order dated 09.05.2007 passed by the High Court of Madhya Pradesh at Jabalpur in Writ Appeal No. 171 of 2006 whereby the Division Bench of the High Court dismissed the appeal filed by the Appellant preferred against the judgment and order dated 20.04.2006 of the Single Judge of the High Court in Writ Petition No. 3842 of 2002 by which the Single Judge dismissed the writ petition of the Appellant wherein the challenge was to the order dated 20.03.2001 passed by the Chief Manager, Bank of India (Respondent No. 3 herein) imposing the punishment of reduction of his basic pay by five stages on the Appellant.

Held, while dismissing the appeal

i. The Scheme is partly mandatory and partly directory. In other words, it is mandatory in compliance of some clauses so far as the employee is concerned, whereas it is directory in compliance of some clauses so far as the Bank is concerned.
ii. In other words, it is not mandatory for the Bank to necessarily complete all the formalities before the due date specified in the clause and if the Bank fails to do it within the time but completes the formalities after the specified date, it would be permissible for the Bank to do so and the act so done would be regarded as being in conformity with the requirement of the Scheme.
iii. Firstly, the Scheme does not provide any consequence as to what would follow, if the Bank does not ensure compliance within the time fixed in the clause. Secondly, the Appellant being a private individual, if he is required to do some act within a specified time prescribed in the Scheme then it is mandatory for him to do so within the time specified. Thirdly, the Bank being a public functionary is required to perform public functions and hence while discharging such functions, if the Scheme has not provided any consequence for non-compliance of the act within time, then the Scheme would not be construed as mandatory but it would be construed as directory insofar as the Bank is concerned. Fourthly, since the Scheme has not provided for accrual of any benefit

in employee's favour by "deeming fiction" in the event of non-compliance on the part of the Bank then no such benefit can accrue in favour of an employee automatically by fiction as a result of any non-compliance. In other words, when the Scheme has provided passing of a specific order by the Bank for accepting the application for voluntary retirement then the application cannot be held as accepted by "deeming fiction".

iv. The Bank was within its rights to issue a charge-sheet to the Appellant on 02.03.2001 because firstly, on 02.03.2001, the Appellant was in the employment of the Bank and, therefore, he could be subjected to face disciplinary proceedings as per the Rules. Secondly, since the memo was served on the Appellant prior to introduction of the Scheme, the disciplinary proceedings were rightly initiated by serving a charge-sheet on the Appellant after coming into force of the Scheme on 01.11.2000. Thirdly, in terms of the Scheme, the Appellant's application could be considered only after conclusion of disciplinary proceedings and, therefore, the Bank was right in considering the application and eventually accepting it on 19.06.2001. Fourthly, the relationship of employee and employer between the Appellant and the Bank continued till 19.06.2001 and, therefore, the Bank was within its rights to take any action under the service rules against the Appellant up to 19.06.2001. It is not in dispute that the Bank took all the disciplinary actions prior to 19.06.2001 and then accepted the application for voluntary retirement on 19.06.2001. Such action, in our view, was just, legal and proper.

v. The Appellant admitted the charges leveled against him in the charge-sheet, there was no need for the Bank to have held any inquiry into the charges. When the charges stood proved on admission of the Appellant, the Bank was justified in imposing punishment on the Appellant as prescribed in the Rules. We, therefore, find no ground to interfere in the punishment order as we also find that having regard to the nature and gravity of the charge, the punishment imposed on the Appellant appears to be just and proper, calling no interference therein.

XIII

Madhya Pradesh State Road Transport Corporation Vs. Manoj Kumar and Ors., 2016

Hon'ble Judges/Coram:

A.K. Sikri and R.K. Agrawal, JJ.

Equivalent Citation: 2017 3 AWC2371SC, 2016(III)CLR620, [2016(151)FLR60], 2016(3)JLJ122, 2016(3)KLJ819, (2016)IVLLJ1SC, 2016(8)SCALE292, (2016)9SCC375, (2016)2SCC(LS)636, 2016 (8) SCJ 645, 2016(4)SCT491(SC), 2016(6)SLR57(SC), MANU/SC/0959/2016

Relevant sections: Clause 4(1)of VoluntaryRetirement from Service Scheme 2005

Number of pages in original Judgment: 14

Case Note:

Service - Voluntary Retirement Scheme - Request for withdrawal - Applicability of date - Respondents/employees' requests for withdrawal of their option were not entertained - On contrary applications for VRS submitted by these employees were accepted - Single Judge of High Court dismissed petitions of these employees - It was held that applications for withdrawal of VRS could only be moved within validity period of Scheme - Appeals came to be filed before Division Bench of High Court by aggrieved employees - Division Bench decided all these appeals together and allowed them holding that it is always permissible for employee to withdraw option under VRS before it is accepted - Hence, present appeal - Whether validity of Scheme was extended up to July 31, 2007 and employees could withdraw their offer before that date or date on which initial scheme expired, i.e. August 01, 2005 and withdrawal thereafter was not permissible

Brief Facts:

As the Appellant Transport Corporation was running into losses, the State Government obtained permission from the Ministry. Considering the closure of the Corporation, the Managing Director introduced a Scheme called as Voluntary Retirement from Service (VRS) for the employees of the Corporation. The Scheme, it provided certain conditions and also a specific form in which the application/option for VRS under the Scheme was to be made. Further, one of the conditions in the VRS Scheme was that once the application form for opting VRS is submitted, it would not be open to the applicant to withdraw the same. The Respondents/employees had submitted their applications for voluntary retirement within the span of original period fixed under the Scheme, i.e. between July 01, 2005 and August 01, 2005. Other common factor in all these appeals was that before their applications could be accepted, they had sought withdrawal of their option. However, requests for withdrawal of the options were made after August 01, 2005, i.e. after the expiry of the original Scheme. However, their requests for withdrawal were not entertained and on the contrary applications for VRS submitted by these employees were accepted. These Respondents challenged the aforesaid action by contending that once they had withdrawn their application for VRS, there was no question of going ahead with the option of VRS and accepting the same. Therefore, the action of the Corporation was unwarranted and contrary to law. All these employees approached the High Court and filed respective writ petitions challenging the aforesaid action of the Corporation. The Single Judge of the High Court dismissed these writ petitions. It was held that the applications for withdrawal of VRS could only be moved within the validity period of the Scheme and in those cases where applications for withdrawal was submitted after August 01, 2005, this could not be done by the concerned employees. Writ appeals came to be filed before the Division Bench of the High Court by the aggrieved employees. The Division Bench, vide the impugned judgment, decided all these appeals together and allowed them holding that it is always permissible for an employee to withdraw the option under VRS before it is accepted. The High

Court has proceeded on the basis that such a VRS Scheme calling for options is an invitation to offer. Application submitted by an employee opting under this Scheme qua voluntary retirement amounts to an officer and only on the acceptance of such an offer by the employee, a deal gets concluded and such an offer can, therefore, always be withdrawn before it is accepted. Hence, the present appeal.

Held, while allowing the petition: :

i. In those cases where the Scheme is contractual in nature, provisions of the Indian Contract Act would apply. The VRS Scheme floated by the employer would be treated as invitation to offer and the application submitted by the employees pursuant thereto is an offer which does not amount to resignation in praesenti and the offer can be withdrawn during the validity period. This would be the position even when there is a Clause in the Scheme that offer once given cannot be withdrawn at all. However, exception to this principle is that in such cases offer is to be withdrawn during the validity period of the Scheme and not thereafter even when if it is not accepted during the period of the Scheme.
ii. The Corporation had floated the Scheme because of the reason that it has virtually stopped transport business and the purpose of the Scheme was to benefit itself by shrinking the strength of the employees as with no transport business need for such employees is not there. Here also, the Scheme provided that once the option is given, the same cannot be withdrawn. Notwithstanding this clause, the employees had a right to withdraw the offer during the validity period but not thereafter. This legal principle was even taken note of by the High Court as well in the impugned judgment. The High Court, however, held that though the Scheme was valid up to August 01, 2005, but validity was extended up to July 31, 2007, the employees could withdraw their offers before July 31, 2007. Further, as in all these cases where the offer was withdrawn before July 31, 2007, the High Court dismissed the appeals of the Corporation.
iii. Acceptance of offer after the withdrawal would be of no consequence. However, those employees who withdrew their offers after August 01, 2005 could not do so and, therefore, the Corporation was within its right to accept their offers. Likewise, those employees belonging to the second category who had withdrawn their offers before October 28, 2006 were entitled to withdraw their offers as those were not accepted by that

date. However, the withdrawal after October 28, 2006 when Scheme was closed would be of no consequence.

iv. Insofar as those employees who fall in the first category are concerned, they had withdrawn their offer after August 01, 2005, except one Respondent No. 1. Therefore, from this batch, only he was entitled for reinstatement with back wages, as he has also filed an undertaking, in terms of this Court's order, to the effect that he was not gainfully employed during the relevant period. Likewise, employees falling in the second category had withdrawn their offer after October 28, 2006, except two Respondents. However, these Respondents failed to comply with this Court's order. They were, therefore, entitled for reinstatement without back wages. The direction of the High Court reinstating these Respondents/employees was, therefore, found to be contrary to law and was hereby set aside, resulting into allowing all other appeals of the Corporation.

XIV

Assistant General Manager, State Bank of India and Ors. Vs. Radhey Shyam Pandey and Ors., 2015

Hon'ble Judges/Coram:

V. Gopala Gowda and Dipak Misra, JJ.

Equivalent Citation: 2015(3)SCALE39, (2015)12SCC451, (2016)1SCC(LS)406, 2015 (4) SCJ 93, 2015(2)SCT263(SC), MANU/SC/0197/2015

Relevant sections: Clause 22(i)(a) of Pension Fund Rules, 1995; Rule 22 of State Bank of India Employees Pension Rules; Articles 12 and 39 of Constitution of India, 1950

Number of pages in original Judgment: 29

Case Note:

Service - Pension benefits - Entitlement thereto - Clause 22(i)(a) of Pension Fund Rules, 1995 - Present appeals filed against order whereby, Respondents were allowed pension as per Rules under Clause 22(i)(a) - Whether employees who had not completed specified number of years in service were entitled to pension - Held, there was no provision for computation of broken period - Unless employee had completed specified number of years in service he would not be entitled to pension - Therefore employees who had not completed specified number of years in service were not entitled to pension - Appeal allowed.

Service - Pension benefits - Entitlement thereto - Rule 22 of State Bank of India Employees Pension Rules - Present appeals filed against order whereby, Respondent was held to be entitled to pension in terms of Rule 22 of Rules - Whether Respondent-employees were entitled to pension benefits under Rule 22(i)(c) of Rules alone - Held, incentives of Scheme were distinct from benefits provided under Rule 22(i)(c) of Rules - Clause 6(c) of Scheme did not specifically state that pension benefits were to be provided under Rule 22(i)(c) of Rules - Therefore claim for pension by Respondent could not be decided solely on basis of provision of Rule 22(1)(c) of Rules - Appeals disposed of.

Service - Employment Rules - Entitlement thereto - Articles 12 and 39 of Constitution of India, 1950 - Whether State Bank of India was entitled to retain its own employment Rules which were not in consonance with subsequent amendments - Held, in setting up schemes Appellant Bank which was instrumentality of State under Article 12 of Constitution could not deviate from its constitutional duties - Appellant Bank decision to distinguish between two sets of employees was against Article 39 of Constitution which directed policies to ensure equal pay for equal work - Appellant being instrumentality of State was not permitted to make such discrimination - Therefore, Appellant was liable to implement amendments made by Association and to accommodate grant of pension to employees who had sought voluntary retirement - Appeals disposed of.

Brief Facts:

i. Having regard to the commonality of controversy in this batch of appeals it was heard together and is disposed of by a singular judgment. For the sake of clarity and convenience, I shall adumbrate the facts from Civil Appeal Nos. 2287-2288 of 2010 and at the appropriate stage refer to the views expressed in other appeals. The 1st Respondent, M.P. Hallan, an ex-serviceman joined as a clerk on 18.5.1981 in the Appellant-Bank which has been constituted under the State Bank of India Act, 1955 (for brevity 'the Act'). The Indian Banks Association (I.B.A.), after obtaining approval from the Government of India evolved a Voluntary Retirement Scheme (V.R.S.) and the Appellant-Bank adopted the Scheme with certain modifications, despite it having its own Voluntary Retirement Scheme in the existing service conditions meant for its employees to seek voluntary retirement/premature retirement/resignation. The Scheme, namely, S.B.I. Voluntary Retirement Scheme (for short 'the Scheme') was adopted by the State Bank of India on 29.12.2000. The Scheme was to remain open during the period 15.1.2001 to 31.1.2001 with the option either to close it early or extend the period, without assigning any reason.

ii. After adoption of the Scheme, the Deputy Managing Director, the competent authority, issued a Circular No. HRD/CDO/VRS/1 on 29.12.2000 clarifying certain aspects of the Scheme. Another Circular being No. HRD/CDO/VRS/5 was issued on 10.1.2001. On 11.01.2001, the said Circular was brought to the notice of all the Branches/offices of all the Circles, including Chandigarh Circle.

iii. As per the Scheme, the applications for voluntary retirement under the Scheme were to be submitted during the period i.e. 15.1.2001 to 31.1.2001. The 1st Respondent submitted his application seeking voluntary retirement and it was accepted on 17.3.2001 with effect from 31.3.2001. On 27.3.2001, the Respondent No. 1 submitted an application to withdraw his request for voluntary retirement. The said application was declined by the Bank on 18.4.2001 stating that the date for withdrawal of application had already expired on 15.2.2001. It is apt to note that here the Respondent wrote a letter on 12.4.2001 claiming pension under the Pension Fund Rules, 1995 in terms of State Bank of India Employees Pension Rules (for short 'the Rules'). The claim of the 1st Respondent for withdrawal of his application for voluntary retirement and grant of pension and leave encashment was refused by the Bank on 4.7.2001. Being grieved by the aforesaid refusal and declination of the prayer, the 1st Respondent preferred writ petition being CWP No. 14325 of 2001.

iv. The Writ Court took note of the fact there was acceptance of the voluntary retirement on 17.3.2001 with a stipulation that the employee would be relieved from his duties at the close of business hours on 31.3.2001. The Division Bench referred to the decision in Mohinder Pal Singh v. Punjab and Sind Bank and Ors. 2002 (2) SLR 716 and the decision of this Court in Bank of India and Ors. v. O.P. Swarankar etc. MANU/SC/1179/2002 : (2003) 2 SCC 721 and after reproducing the directions of from Swarankar's case came to hold as follows:

In view of the aforesaid finding, the moment a decision is taken by the Bank, the jural relationship of employer and employee stood terminated. The Petitioner has admittedly sought to withdraw his offer to seek voluntary retirement after the acceptance was conveyed to the Petitioner. Mere fact that the date of voluntary retirement was fixed as 31.03.2001, is wholly inconsequential as employer and employee relationship has already come to an end with the communication of acceptance. It was only the procedural part under which the Petitioner continued to work till 31.03.2001.

i. In the ultimate analysis, the High Court did not find any merit with regard to refusal by the Bank in not accepting the application for withdrawal submitted by the employee. Determination on the said score is not under assail in any of the appeals before this Court.
ii. The next question that emerged for consideration before the High Court was whether the employee was entitled to pension in terms of the rules, including computed value of pension. It was contended by the 1st Respondent in the writ court that the pension rules were amended on 9.3.2001 and the said rules were in vogue when the Petitioner had submitted his application for voluntary retirement, and hence, he was entitled to get the pensionary benefits. It was also urged that in terms of the amended Rule 22 of the pension rules, he was entitled to pension. The said submission was resisted by the Bank that Rule 22 did not cover the cases like that of the Petitioner. In justification of the said submission, reliance was placed on the Division Bench judgment of the High Court of Delhi in Vipin Kalia and Ors. v. State Bank of India and Ors. decided on 28.2.2007 in L.P.A. No. 410 of 2002 and also on a decision rendered by the High Court of Andhra Pradesh in C.W.P. No. 2098 of 2006.

Held, while disposing off the petitions:

i. The amendment in Regulation 28, as is reflected from the afore referred communication, was intended to cover the employees who had rendered 15 years' service but not completed 20 years' service....
ii. Even if it be assumed that by insertion of the proviso in Regulation 28 (in the year 2002 with effect from 1-9-2000), all classes of employees under VRS, 2002 were intended to be covered, such amendment in Regulation 28, needs to be harmonized with Regulation 29....
iii. While answering Point no, 2 in favour of the Respondents, I held that the State Bank of India should implement the amendment made to Rule 28 of the Employees Pension Regulation in granting pension to the employees seeking voluntary retirement under SBI-VRS.

iv. I therefore, answer point No. 3 in favour of the Respondents and direct the Appellant Bank to grant pension to the employees seeking voluntary retirement under the SBI-VRS after completing 15 years of pensionable service. Therefore, the Respondent Radhey Shyam Pandey, having completed 19 years 8 months and 18 days of service, Respondent M.P. Hallan, having completed 19 years and 4 months of service and the Respondent R.P. Nigam, having completed 16 years and 6 months of service, become eligible for pension as per the amended Regulation 28 of Employees Pension Rules, 1995. By virtue of power vested in this Court Under Article 142 Constitution of India, I hold that the pension relief is also extended to all the other employees who have availed SBI-VRS 2000 after having completed 15 years of pensionable service. Thus, C.A. No. @ SLP (C) No. 3686 of 2007, C.A. Nos. 2287-2288 of 2010 and C.A. No. 10813 of 2013 are dismissed.

v. The C.A. Nos. 5035-5037 of 2012 of the Appellant Bank succeed in that Respondent Mihir Kumar Nandi, having completed 12 years 3 months and 4 days of service, becomes ineligible for pension benefits.

vi. All the appeals are disposed of accordingly. No costs.

XV

Senior Divisional Manager Life Insurance Corporation of India Ltd. and Ors. Vs. Lal Meena, 2015

Hon'ble Judges/Coram:

Dipak Misra and Prafulla C. Pant, JJ.

Equivalent Citation: AIR2016SC1394, 2016(3)BLJ75, [2016(149)FLR609], 2016LabIC2151, 2016(2)SCALE526, (2015)17SCC43, 2016(2)SCT312(SC), 2016(6)SLR194(SC), MANU/SC/1566/2015

Relevant sections: Rules 3 and 34 of Life Insurance Corporation (Employees) Pension Rules, 1995

Number of pages in original Judgment: 14

Case Note:

Service - Retiral benefits - Applicability thereof - Voluntary retired employee - Rules 3 and 34 of Life Insurance Corporation (Employees) Pension Rules, 1995 - Present Appeal filed against order of High Court granting retiral benefits to Respondent-Employee on basis of Rules, 1995 - Whether Respondent was rightly ranted retiral benefits

Brief Facts:

The present appeal, by special leave, is directed against the judgment and order dated 16.08.2011 passed by the Division Bench of the Rajasthan High Court at Jaipur Bench in D.B. Civil Special Appeal (Writ) No. 172 of 2008 in S.B. Civil Writ Petition No. 6026 of 1997 wherein the writ Court had allowed the Writ Petition preferred by the Respondent-employee, for grant of retiral benefits from the Life Insurance Corporation of India Ltd. (for brevity, "the Corporation") on the basis of the Life Insurance Corporation (Employees) Pension Rules, 1995.

Held, while referring the matter before larger bench

i. The 1995 Rules has been given retrospective effect on two scores, namely, the provisions will apply retrospectively with effect from the 1st day of November, 1993; and even employees who retired after the 1st day of January, 1986 and before the 1st day of November, 1993 could be entitled to exercise option to be covered under the pension scheme, subject to stipulated pre-conditions. We have already referred to Rule 3 of the 1995 Rules. As is demonstrable, the retiring employees who had been paid provident fund had to exercise their option and refund the amount paid with interest within the requisite time frame. Appreciated in this manner, it is obvious that the 1995 Rules do not postulate and do not give liberty/right to the retiring employees covered by Rule 3 to exercise option at any time. The window period and pre-conditions were specific and mandatory.
ii. Prior to enforcement of the aforesaid Rules, there was no concept in the Corporation which pertained to voluntary retirement. Section 2(s) of the 1995 Rules refers to voluntary retirement in accordance with the provisions contained in Rule 31 of the 1995 Rules. Rule 31 has not been given retrospective operation and effect. The retrospective operation of the 1995 Rules in entirety is limited to the employees, who had retired in normal course of superannuation. Needless to say, resignation has the effect of termination of an employee. Voluntary retirement though has the effect of termination of employee yet it has different consequences. In the former case, the ex-employee could not be entitled to pension, whereas in case of voluntary retirement, the latter one, the employee would be entitled to pension depending upon the terms postulated in the Regulations or rules or the scheme. Rule 23 of the 1995 Rules specifically provides that on resignation, dismissal, removal, termination or

compulsory retirement, the employee shall forfeit the entire past service and he shall not qualify for pensionary benefit. Thus, resignation given under the 1995 Rules would not entitle an employee to get pension.

iii. We may further note here that whether an employee can take voluntary retirement would depend upon the conditions of employment and the rules applicable to the scheme of voluntary retirement. When Rule 31 was not in operation, the question would arise whether the benefit can be given to an employee who had retired from service. Be it noted that the 1995 Rules are not entirely retrospective. They have limited retrospectivity. Rule 31 expressly has not been made retrospective. Retrospectivity creates a given fiction and, therefore, unless there is express provision or it can be impliedly inferred from the plain and unambiguous language used, a provision should not be given retrospectivity.

iv. To arrive at the real meaning, it is always necessary to understand the scope and object of the whole enactment or the rules. In the said context, the relevant factors are general scope and purview of the statute; remedy sought to be achieved; former state of law and what was contemplated. Unless these conditions are satisfied, it is difficult to treat Rule 31 of the 1995 Rules as retrospective, in the absence of any deemed clause that the employees who had earlier resigned shall be treated as employees as if they had voluntarily retired. In fact, if such an interpretation is placed on the said Rule, it will be travelling beyond the language employed therein.

v. In view of the aforesaid analysis, let the matter be placed before Hon'ble Chief Justice of India for constitution of a larger Bench. Till the matter is decided, the Life Insurance Corporation, the Appellant herein, shall go on paying fifty per cent of the pensionary amount to the Respondent.

XVI

Exide Industries Ltd. Vs. Union of India (UOI) and Ors., 2015

Hon'ble Judges/Coram:

Anil R. Dave and S.K. Singh, JJ.

Equivalent Citation: 2015II AD (S.C.) 635, MANU/SC/0266/2015

Relevant sections: Article 14 Constitution of India, 1950

Number of pages in original Judgment: 08

Case Note:

Service - Voluntary retirement - Petitioners took option of voluntary retirement scheme from Insurance companies in 2004 - Insurance companies released notification revising pay in 2005 - Pay revised with retrospective effect from 2002 - Petitioners claimed benefits of revised pay prior to voluntary retirement - Whether after acceptance of voluntary retirement the Petitioners are entitled to get benefit of pay revised with retrospective effect Constitution - Discrimination - Article 14 Constitution of India, 1950 - Petitioners retired from employ of Insurance companies - Pay raise restricted to employees on or after 2002 - Denied to Petitioners retired in 2004 - Whether not giving the Petitioners the benefit of pay raise is violative of Article 14 Constitution - Whether there was a violation of principle of equal pay for equal work Facts Insurance companies in financial difficulty, to cut expenditure by reducing number of employees, framed scheme for voluntary retirement in 2004, to enable its employees to retire prematurely on certain conditions with some special benefits in addition to normal retirement benefits.

Brief Facts:

Petitioners opted for voluntary retirement in 2004. In 2005, the Insurance companies revised the pay scales of their employees, giving the benefit of increased of pay retrospectively, from 2002. This was subject to employees being in service on or after 2002. The Petitioners demanded a revision of pension under the voluntary retirement scheme, in keeping with pay revised with retrospective effect. The Insurance companies denied the benefit of retrospective increase in pay to the Petitioners, as they had retired under the voluntary scheme. The High Court of Gujarat took a view that the Petitioners had retired under the voluntary scheme were not entitled to any benefit of pay rise. The High Court of Himachal Pradesh held that the Petitioners had retired under the voluntary scheme were entitled to the benefit of pay revision. Hence, the present petition.

Held, while dismissing the petition:

i. The Petitioners, who had taken benefit under the voluntary retirement scheme in 2004, had already retired and would not be entitled to additional pension due to retrospective increase in pay. Normally, retrospective rise in salary is given to those who are in service at the relevant time or who had retired in normal circumstances. The Petitioners had opted under the voluntary scheme, had not retired as per the normal conditions of service but had retired under the scheme, upon taking some special additional benefits.

ii. In normal circumstances when an employee retires from service, his relationship with the employer comes to an end. It is also well settled that after retirement, normally no disciplinary action can, be initiated against the concerned employee. Similarly, the retired employee would not have any right of redetermination of his pension but only in cases where salary is revised with retrospective effect, the retired employee gets the benefit of additional pension and that too in certain cases.

iii. That the pay rise was not given by the Insurance companies to the Petitioners is not discriminatory in nature. The Petitioners who retired under the scheme form a separate class of employees who were given many benefits, which are not given to employees retiring in normal course. If the Petitioners form a separate class, it could not be said that all those who retired under the scheme and those who retired in normal course are similarly situated. Thus, there is no violation of Article 14 of the Constitution. There is also no violation of the principle of equal pay for equal work. The Petitioners received substantially higher retirement benefits.

XVII

P. Krishna Murthy Vs. The Commissioner of Sericulture Andhra Pradesh, 2014

Hon'ble Judges/Coram:

J.S. Khehar and M.Y. Eqbal, JJ.

Equivalent Citation: AIR2014SC3774, 2015(1)ALD37, 2015(2)ALLMR(SC)484, 2014(3)ESC397(SC), [2014(142)FLR813], JT2014(8)SC579, 2014LabIC4148, 2014(4)LLN1(SC), 2014(8)SCALE388, (2014)12SCC549, 2015 (6) SCJ 103, 2014(3)SCT644(SC), 2015(1)SLR510(SC), MANU/SC/0594/2014

Relevant sections: Rule 43 of A.P. Revised Pension Rules, 1980

Number of pages in original Judgment: 05

Case Note:

Service - Reinstatement - Validity of - Present appeal filed against order whereby High court set aside reinstatement order passed in favour of Appellant - Whether reinstatement order was rightly set aside - Held, Evident that after request for revocation of withdrawal of voluntary retirement was rejected, Appellant instead of challenging said order filed several representations for release of pensionary benefits - Said representations were considered and eligible pensionary benefits were drawn and paid to Appellant in 2004 and 2005 - Taking advantage of leniency shown by Government, Appellant took chance to move application after two years requesting authorities for reinstatement in service - Therefore, impugned order of High court in setting aside of reinstatement order was maintainable and required no interference - Appeal dismissed.

Brief Facts:

i. The Appellant at the relevant time was working as Superintendent in the office of Commissioner of Sericulture at Hyderabad. According to the Appellant, sometime in the year 2003, his wife fell sick with onset of menopause stage and mental imbalance and became unable to move. On the allegation against the Appellant that he neglected in discharging his duties, a disciplinary proceeding was initiated on 18.1.2004 and a charge memo was issued. On 3.2.2004, Appellant submitted a representation requesting the Respondent authorities to permit him to retire from service w.e.f. 1.5.2004. On the basis of said representation, the Appellant was permitted to retire from service w.e.f. 1.5.2004 and an order to that effect was issued by the Commissioner, Sericulture dated 4.3.2004.

ii. In purported exercise of power of Rule 43(1) of Andhra Pradesh Revised Pension Rules, 1980, the Appellant's case was that vide application dated 15.4.2004 he requested the authorities to permit him to continue in service till age of superannuation and to revoke the order issued on 4.3.2004. The said application was rejected by the Commissioner, Sericulture vide order dated 28.4.2004. In the meantime, the Commissioner, Sericulture passed an order on 29.7.2004 imposing punishment of 25% cut in the pension amount of the Appellant on the charges of gross negligence in discharging duties. The Appellant challenged the said order dated 29.7.2004 by filing an appeal before the State Government. The said appeal was allowed by the State Government vide order dated 3.4.2006 and the order of Commissioner, Sericulture imposing 25% cut in pension amount was set aside. After the said order was passed by the State Government, the Appellant filed another application on 27.4.2006 seeking issuance of appropriate order for his reinstatement. However, the said application/representation was rejected by the Government vide order dated 1.9.2006. The Appellant challenged the said order before the Administrative Tribunal by filing O.A. No. 6325 of 2006. In the said O.A. an interim order was passed by the Tribunal directing the Appellate Authority of the Respondent to reconsider the case of the Appellant for reinstatement. Pursuant to the said direction, the Government considered the case of the Appellant and finally passed an order on 24.11.2006 holding that the request of the Appellant for reinstatement cannot be considered.

Held, while dismissing the appeal:

i. The aforesaid appeal against the order of 25% cut in pension, the State Government considered it sympathetically and allowed the appeal and set aside the order of imposing penalty and directed to drop the proceedings against the Appellant, who is a retired officer. It is also worth to mention here that after his request for revocation of withdrawal of voluntary retirement was finally rejected, the Appellant instead of challenging the said order filed several representations for release of the pensionary benefits. The said representations were considered and the eligible pensionary benefits were drawn and paid to the Appellant in 2004 and 2005. Taking advantage of the leniency shown by the Government in the order passed in appeal on 3.4.2004, the Appellant took a chance to move an application after two years i.e. on 27.4.2006 requesting the authorities for reinstatement in service.
ii. In these factual backgrounds of the instant case, we are of the considered opinion that the principles laid down in **Balram Gupta's case and S.N. Srivastava's case** (supra) are not applicable and are distinguishable. The High Court in the impugned order has rightly came to the conclusion that the Appellant preferred appeal before the State Government against the impugned order of cut in pension as a retired employee and he himself stated that he has submitted the pension proposals for fixation of pension. Besides the above, we are further of the opinion that having regard to the fact that the Appellant did not assail the order rejecting his application for revocation of pension at any time rather he proceeded and assailed only the order of 25% cut in pension. Hence, the Appellant cannot be allowed to proceed further, that too after expiry of two years seeking reinstatement in service taking the benefit of the order passed by the State Government.
iii. In the aforesaid circumstances, we do not find any error in the impugned order passed by the High Court. There is no merit in these appeals, which are accordingly dismissed with no order as to costs.

XVIII

State of Bank of Patiala Vs. Pritam Singh Bedi, 2014

Hon'ble Judges/Coram:

S.J. Mukhopadhaya and V. Gopala Gowda, JJ.

Equivalent Citation: AIR2014SC2714, 2014(3)AJR823, 2014 (4) AWC 4038 (SC), 2014(3)CLJ(SC)38, 2014(III)CLR10, 2014(3)J.L.J.R.426, JT2014(8)SC182, 2014LabIC3146, (2014)IIILLJ513SC, 2014(3)LLN17(SC), 2014(4)PLJR1, 2014(8)SCALE397, (2014)13SCC474, (2015)1SCC(LS)414, 2014 (7) SCJ 181, 2014(3)SCT685(SC), 2014(3)SLJ251(SC), MANU/SC/0588/2014

Relevant sections: Regulations 14, 18 and 29 of State Bank of Patiala (Employees) Pension Regulations, 1995

Number of pages in original Judgment: 08

Case Note:

Service - Entitlement to pension - Regulations 14,18 and 29 of State Bank of Patiala (Employees) Pension Regulations, 1995 - Present appeal filed against order whereby Appellant-authority was directed to release pension in favour of Respondents in accordance with State Bank of Patiala Voluntary Retirement Scheme, 2000 - Whether under State Bank of Patiala (Employees) Pension Regulations, 1995, Respondents were entitled for pension - Held, as per scheme Respondents who had completed more than 19 and 1/2 years of service applied for and were allowed to Voluntary Retirement Scheme and they had been paid most of benefits - Evident that

Respondents completed more than 10 years of service in Bank on date of retirement and therefore, they fulfill requirement of qualifying service as per Regulation 14 - Regulation 18 Regulations provides that if broken period is more than six months, it shall be treated as one year - Therefore, all Respondents had completed more than 19 years and 6 months of service in Bank, they were to be treated to have completed 20 years of service - Therefore, Respondents having completed 20 years of service were entitled to benefit of Regulation 29 and entitled to pension - Appeal dismissed.

Brief Facts:

i. All these appeals have been preferred by the State Bank of Patiala (hereinafter referred to as "Bank") against different judgments and orders passed by Punjab and Haryana High Court at Chandigarh but since common issues were involved they were heard together and disposed of by the impugned common judgment.

ii. A number of employees who were allowed to retire from the Bank pursuant to scheme called State Bank of Patiala Voluntary Retirement Scheme, 2000(herein after referred to as the "Scheme") introduced by Circular dated 20th January, 2001, and had completed more than 19 and 1/2 years of service, in whose favour pension was not released by the Bank in accordance with the State Bank of Patiala (Employees) Pension Regulations, 1995 (hereinafter referred to as the "Regulations, 1995"). They moved before the High Court for direction to the Bank and its authorities to release pension in their favour in accordance with the Scheme. By one of the judgments dated 22nd October, 2008, learned Single Judge of the High Court allowed the writ petitions preferred by some of the aggrieved employees (Respondents) in C.A. No. 172 of 2010 and directed to pay pension in their favour. Against the said order the Bank preferred LPA No. 312 of 2008 before the Division Bench, which by the impugned judgment dated 9th January, 2009 dismissed the LPA and affirmed the order passed by the learned Single Judge. The said impugned judgment dated 9th January, 2009 passed in LPA No. 312 of 2008 is under challenge in C.A. No. 172 of 2010.

iii. Some other similarly situated employees who had completed more than 19 and 1/2 years of service and retired persons to Voluntary Retirement Scheme also preferred similar writ petitions which were allowed. Against the respective judgments Bank filed different LPAs which were also dismissed by different orders in view of the judgment dated 9th January,

2009. Against the judgments which have followed the earlier decision, the rest of the civil appeals have been preferred by the Bank.

Held, while dismissing the petition:

i. The Respondents completed more than 10 years of service in the Bank on the date of retirement; therefore, they fulfill the requirement of qualifying service as per Regulation 14.

ii. It has not been disputed by Appellant-Bank that the Respondents in all the appeals have completed much more than 19 years 6 months of service in the Bank. For example, Respondent No. 1-Prakash Chand in C.A. No. 173 of 2010 had joined the Bank on 4th May, 1981 and relieved on 31st March, 2001. Thus, he had completed 19 years, 10 months and 28 days of qualifying service on the date of relieving from service.

iii. Regulation 18 of the Pension Regulations, 1995 provides that if broken period is more than six months, it shall be treated as one year. Therefore, all the Respondents-writ Petitioners having completed more than 19 years and 6 months of service in the Bank, they are to be treated to have completed 20 years of service. The aforesaid question was neither raised nor decided in the case of ***'Bank of Baroda' or 'Bank of India'***.

iv. In view of the aforesaid fact, the Appellant-Bank cannot derive the benefit of the decision of this Court in ***Bank of Baroda*** as the employees who were parties before the Court in the said case had not completed 20 years of service. As per the decision of this Court in ***Bank of India***, the Respondents-writ Petitioners having completed 20 years of service are entitled to the benefit of Regulation 29.

v. In view of the finding recorded above, the appeals do not have merit in reference with the impugned judgment, they are, accordingly, dismissed. No costs.

XIX

Union of India (UOI) and Ors. Vs. Ajay Wahi

Hon'ble Judges/Coram:

G.S. Singhvi and C.K. Prasad, JJ.

Equivalent Citation: AIR2010SC2603, 2010(5)ALLMR(SC)471, 2010 6 AWC5570SC, 2010(3)BLJ156, [2010(126)FLR904], JT2010(6)SC411, 2010LabIC3102, (2010)6MLJ421(SC), 2010(6)SCALE282, (2010)11SCC213, 2010(3)SCT354(SC), 2010(4)SLR368(SC), 2010(4)SLR368(SC), 2010(7)UJ3482, MANU/SC/0429/2010

Relevant sections: Regulations 48 and 50 Pension Regulation, 1995

Number of pages in original Judgment: 06

Ratio Decidendi:

"No disability pension to be granted in cases of voluntary retirements under Regulation 50 of the Pension Rules."

Case Note:

Service - Voluntary Retirement - Demand of Disability Pension - Grant thereof - Challenge against thereto - Regulations 48 and 50 Pension Regulation, 1995 - Respondent sought premature retirement from army on medical grounds, inter alia, stating that his "falling health is affecting" his performance - Respondent's retirement was approved but his claim for disability pension was rejected - Aggrieved by the denial of disability pension he filed writ petition before the High Court which was dismissed by the Single Judge but subsequently allowed by Division Bench - Hence present appeal - Whether Respondents were entitled for payment of disability pension - Held, An officer who retires voluntarily and another who is invalided out of service on account of disability attributable to military service constitute different and distinct classes - An officer is entitled for disability pension only when he is invalided out of service on account of disability attributable to military service or aggravated thereby - In the present case, Respondent sought voluntary retirement on medical ground and, therefore, cannot be said to be invalided out of service on account of disability attributable to or aggravated by military service - Provision of the Statute can be declared ultravires only when it patently violates some provision of the Constitution - Regulation 50 does not suffer from any such error - Thus, in view of Regulation 50 of Pension Regulations, Respondents having retired voluntarily shall not be eligible for award of pension on account of any disability - Appeal allowed

Brief Facts:

Shorn of unnecessary details, facts giving rise to this appeal are that the writ petitioner-respondent, Lt. Col. Ajay Wahi (hereinafter referred to as the 'writ petitioner') was commissioned in the Army Medical Corps on 27th February, 1977. While in service and holding the rank of Major he was admitted to Command Hospital on 3rd October, 1988 for management and treatment of Bronchial Asthma and low back ache. Medical Board proceeding dated 6th October, 1988 does not indicate that the disability i.e. Bronchial Asthma or low back ache was directly attributable to military service. However, the Medical Board certified that it is aggravated by stress and strain of exposure to hostile terrain and weather. The writ petitioner was later on examined on 9th June, 1990 by Col. T.R.S. Bedi, Senior Adviser of Base Hospital who recommended for his posting at dry temperate climate area and not at high altitude. While writ petitioner was holding the rank of Lieutenant Colonel, by letter dated 27th December, 1993, he sought premature retirement, inter alia, stating that his "falling health is affecting" his performance. On his prayer for premature retirement the Commanding Officer recommended for consideration of his case for "invalidment/ premature retirement after obtaining the opinion of a Senior Adviser". He was neither called upon to appear before the Medical Board nor invalided on medical ground. However, by order dated 26th July, 1994, writ petitioner's prayer for premature retirement was approved and he was allowed to leave the unit on 20th October, 1994. Writ petitioner made claim for grant of disability pension. His prayer was considered and by letter dated 30th March, 1995, he was informed that he is neither entitled for service pension nor disability pension. Writ petitioner wrote to the Director General of Medical

Services(Army) to make him available the copy of the Medical Board proceedings, inter alia, alleging that he underwent a Release Medical Board prior to retirement. It is assertion of the writ petitioner that he ought to have been granted premature retirement on medical ground and sought voluntary retirement under pressure and, therefore, entitled to disability pension.

Held, while allowing the appeal:

We are of the opinion that an officer is entitled for disability pension only when he is invalided out of service on account of disability attributable to military service or aggravated thereby and shall not be entitled for disability pension in case of voluntary retirement, unless it is found and held that the officer deserved to be invalided out of service on account of disability attributable to military service but the same was not granted to him for unjustified reasons and forced to seek voluntary retirement.

In the result, the appeal is allowed, the impugned judgment of the Division Bench of the High Court is set aside and that of the learned Single Judge is restored. No costs.

XX

M.D. Orissa S.H.W. Coop. Sty. Ltd. Vs. Satyanarayan Pattnaik and Ors., 2014

Hon'ble Judges/Coram:

Anil R. Dave and Dipak Misra, JJ.

Relevant sections: Article 14 and 16 of Constitution of India

Number of pages in original Judgment: 03

Equivalent Citation: 2014 2 AWC1710SC, 2014(2)CDR511(SC), [2014(141)FLR89], 2014(2)LLN316(SC), 2014LLR337, 2014(2)SCALE256, (2014)3SCC218, (2014)2SCC(LS)183, 2014(2)SCT81(SC), 2014(2)SLJ511(SC), 2014(5)SLR709(SC), 2014 (3) WLN 91 (SC), MANU/SC/0115/2014

Case Note:

Employment - Voluntary retirement--Withdrawal--Voluntary retirement scheme floated by appellant-employer--Application for voluntary retirement was accepted though respondent-employee wanted to withdraw same--Respondent-employee filed petition before High Court, which was allowed and High Court, by virtue of impugned judgment, directed that respondent-employee should be taken in service within two months with full back wages--Review petition filed by appellant-employer rejected by High Court--Keeping question of law open, looking at peculiar facts of case appeal of appellant-employer deserves to be allowed to limited extent by directing appellant-employer to pay only 20% of back wages from date when respondent-employee ceased to discharge his duties till date he is reinstated in service--Respondent-employee directed to be reinstated in service.

Brief Facts:

The Respondent was an employee, who had submitted his application for voluntary retirement under the Voluntary Retirement Scheme dated 9.6.2006 floated by the Appellant-employer. Before the final decision in pursuance of the said application was communicated by the Appellant-employer to the Respondent-employee, the Respondent-employee had made a request for withdrawal of the said application and ultimately the Appellant-employer had not accepted the application for withdrawal submitted by the Respondent-employee and the Respondent-employee was made to retire.

Held, while disposing off the petition:

i. In view of the fact that his application for voluntary retirement was accepted though the Respondent-employee wanted to withdraw the same, the Respondent-employee had filed a petition before the High Court, which was allowed and the High Court, by virtue of the impugned judgment, directed that the Respondent-employee should be taken in service within two months with full back wages. Even the review petition filed by the Appellant had been rejected by the High Court.

ii. Keeping the question of law open, looking at the peculiar facts of the case, we feel that the appeal deserves to be allowed to a limited extent by directing the Appellant-employer to pay only 20% of the back wages from the date when the Respondent ceased to discharge his duties till the date he is reinstated in service.

iii. The Respondent shall be reinstated in service within two weeks from today.

iv. In view of the above order, the appeals stand disposed of as partly allowed with no order as to costs.

VIDEOS & TV SHOWS ON LAW & EXIM

List of some important videos & TV shows on Law & EXIM by Adv. Jayprakash Somani on his YouTube Channel 'Jayprakash Somani EXIM & Legal'

Legal Videos: Hindi -English

1) SLP in Supreme Court / Special Leave Petitions in the Supreme Court of India

2) Transfer of Civil & Criminal Cases by the Supreme Court of India / Transfer of Matrimonial Cases

3) Appellate Jurisdiction of the Supreme Court of India

4) Jurisdictions of the Supreme Court of India

5) Public Interest Litigation in the Supreme Court of India / PIL in Supreme Court

6) Article 32 Writ Petitions in the Supreme Court of India

7) Bail Matters Top 10 Supreme Court Cases

8) FIR Quashing in High Court & Supreme Court

9) Bail & Anticipatory Bail Matters in Supreme Court

10) Insolvency & Bankruptcy Matters in the Supreme Court

11) Insolvency & Bankruptcy Code 2016 Part 1

12) Insolvency & Bankruptcy Code 2016 Part 2

13) Insolvency & Bankruptcy Code 2016 Part 3

14) Corporate Liquidation Process

15) Supreme Court Rules & Procedures Webinar of 2.5 hour on Zoom

16) RDDBFI Act, 1993 (Introduction)

17) The Indian Contact Act 1872

18) Negotiable Instruments Act (Introduction)

19) How to avoid matrimonial disputes& some more videos

20)SEBI Matters in the Supreme Court

21) Matrimonial Matters: Supreme Court's 20 Case Laws

22) Consumer Matters Supreme Court's 20 Case Laws

23) Service Matters Supreme Court's 20 Case Laws

24) How to Search Lawyer for Your Matter

25) Property Matters Supreme Court's 20 Case Laws

26) Bail Matters: Supreme Court's 20 Case Laws

27) Supreme Court / High Court Vacation Benches

28)69000 Teacher's Recruitment Matters of UP Government in the Supreme Court

29) Contempt of Court Matters in the Supreme Court

30) Advocate Act's Matters in the Supreme Court

31) Business Law Matters in the Supreme Court

32) Banking Matters in the Supreme Court

33) Labour Law Matters in the Supreme Court

34) Arbitration Matters in the Supreme Court

35) Careers in Law -Zoom Webinar by Adv. Jayprakash Somani

36) Civil Matters in the Supreme Court

37) Consumer Protection Act | Consumer Matters in the Supreme Court

38) Corporate Matters in the Supreme Court

39) Criminal Matters in the Supreme Court

40) Role of Respondent in the Supreme Court of India

41) Motor Vehicle Accident Matters in Supreme Court with case laws

42) Article 131 Original Suits in Supreme Court

43)PIL in Supreme Court/ Public Interest Litigations in the Supreme Court of India'

44)CAB Citizenship Amendment Bill is not Unconstitutional

45) Supreme Court of India Cases & Process – Marathi

46) Legal Services Export / Export of Legal Services

47) Transfer of Matrimonial Cases by the Supreme Court of India

48) Public Interest Litigation PIL

49) The Specific Relief Act (Introduction)

50) Corporate Insolvency Resolution Process CIRP

51)ABMM's Career 5 - Careers in Law

52) Transfer of cases by Supreme Court

53) Writ Petitions in High Court & Supreme Court of India

54) Supreme Court Jurisdictions - Appeals, SLP, Writ Petitions, Transfer, Original, Review, Curative

55)LEGAL INDIA TV Show: Cases Handled in Supreme Court

56) Corporate Liquidation Process

57) Legal Services Export / Export of Legal Services

EXIM Videos: Hindi -English

1) Yes, I can do Import Export Business Easily! 36 points excellent video in Hindi

2) Yes, I can do Import Export Business Easily! 36 points excellent video in English

3) Import Export Business – Hindi video

4) Import Export Business - English video

5) Export Import Marathi TV Interview

6) Scope for Commerce Students in International Business- TV Show

7) Scope for Management Student in International Business- TV Show

8) Scope for Engineering Students in International Business – TV Show

9) Women in International Business- TV Show

10) How to do Import Export Business Successfully!‘

11) Where one can get full information on Import Export Business?

12) What to do import & export?

13) Import Export Workshop/ Training/Course/ Diploma

14) How to Start Import Export Business & How to grow it. Live Webinar

15) Success Stories & Failure Stories in Import & Export Business

16) For MSME Scope in Export & Import...

17) Exports In Agri. & Food Products – English & some more videos

18) Exports to Dubai, Aabudhabii. e. UAE

19) Jewelry Exports from India

20) How to attend EXIM workshop to become excellent Exporter

21) Import Export Best Training Course – Online & Offline

22) Agri Product Export

23) Scope for Woman in International Business

24) Management Graduates Scope in International Business

25) Pharma Product’s Export

26) Best Import Export Course | Practical Training | Aaronica Global Exim

27) Import Export Business for Commerce Graduates

28) How Do I Get Export Orders? Finding International Buyers

29) What Is APEDA In Import Export Business?

30) Which Is The Best Product To Export From India?

31)EXIM Remark by Manoj Kumar Faridabad

32)EXIM Remarks by Mahesh Telangana

33) What Licenses I Need To Start Import/ Export?

34) How Can I Increase My Import Export Business?

35) Which Is Best B2B Website For Import/Export Business?

36) Export Import Management with Global Marketing

37) How to Start Export Import Business | 51 Points Video

38) Scope for Commerce & Other Graduates in International Business

39)BE A SUCCESSFUL EXPORTER FOR OUR NATION - Marathi video

40) Export of Textile , Cotton, Agri., Food, & other products & services

41) Exports from MP, CG, MH, GJ & CA in Fresh Fruits & Vegetables

42) Exports in Agri. & Food Products- Hindi

43) Start your Online/E-Commerce Business

44) How to Start Export Import Business & Grow it

45) Exports in Textile & Other Products

46) Start and grow EXIM business - Live English Webinar

47)'Import Export Business!' Why, Who, What &How can one do it easily!!

48) Live: Export of Product & Services During & After Lock Down Period

49) Frauds in Import Export Business

50) Import Export for Business Man

51) Import& Export for Women

51) Import& Export for Graduate & Post - Graduate Students

52) Agriculture Exports from India

53) Digital Marketing Setup - Marathi

54)2nd Secret of Successful Businessman

55) Digital Marketing Set up

56) Legal Services Export / Export of Legal Services

57) Export& Import with UAE

58) Service Exports / Exports by Service Providers

59) Import Export Workshop/ Training/Course/ Diploma

60) Exports& Imports with USA

61) Selection on Product for Export

62) Top Products Exported from India

63) What to do import & export?

64)ABMM Career 2 - 'Careers in Business & Industries

65) How to do Import Export Business Successfully!'

66)5 Secrets of Successful Businessman

67) Export from MP, Chhattisgarh &Vidarbha Nagpur

68)EXIM Hindi - Textile & Apparel Export

69)EXIM Hindi - Export Import Practical Training In Delhi, Kolkata, Mumbai and Pune

70) Import Export Business

71) Import Export Business Hindi

72) Import Export Business English video

73) Import Export Business Marathi

74) Women in International Business by Exim Guru Adv. Jayprakash Somani

75) Opportunities in Foreign Trade- Adv. Jayprakash Somani's special interview

ꕥ

LIST OF ADV. JAYPRAKASH SOMANI'S BOOKS

1. Supreme Court of India's Leading Case Laws on 'Insolvency & Bankruptcy Code 2016'
2. Bail Matters – Supreme Court's Latest Leading Case Laws
3. Arbitration Matters- Supreme Court's Latest Leading Case Laws
4. Property Matters - Supreme Court's Latest Leading Case Laws
5. Matrimonial Matters- Supreme Court's Latest Leading Case Laws
6. Election Matters- Supreme Court's Latest Leading Case Laws
7.SEBI Matters- Supreme Court's Latest Leading Case Laws
8. Banking Matters- Supreme Court's Latest Leading Case Laws
9. Service Matters- Supreme Court's Latest Leading Case Laws
10. Contempt of Court Matters- Supreme Court's Latest Leading Case Laws
11. Consumer Protection Matters- Supreme Court's Latest Leading Case Laws
12. Corporate Law- Supreme Court's Latest Leading Case Laws
13. Supreme Court's AOR Exam- Leading Cases
14. Armed Force Tribunal - Supreme Court's Latest Leading Case Laws
15. Acquittal From 376 - Supreme Court's Latest Leading Case Laws
16. Negotiable instrument – Supreme Court's Latest Leading Case Laws
17. Contract Act- Supreme Court's Latest Leading Case Laws
18. Insider trading- Supreme Court's Latest Leading Case Laws
19. Foreign Exchange and Management Act- Supreme Court's Latest Leading Case Laws
20. Income Tax Act- Supreme Court's Latest Leading Case Laws
21. Company Law- Supreme Court's Latest Leading Case Laws
22. Competition & Monopoly Matters- Supreme Court's Latest Leading Case Laws
23. Compassionate Appointment- Service Matters- Supreme Court's Latest Leading Case Laws
24. Compulsory Retirement- Service Matters- Supreme Court's Latest Leading Case Laws
25. Voluntary Retirement- Service Matters- Supreme Court's Latest Leading Case Laws

These Books are available online at

1. **Notion Press:**https://notionpress.com/author/jayprakash_somani
2. **Amazon:**https://www.amazon.in/s?k=jayprakash+somani
3. **Flipkart:**https://www.flipkart.com/search?q=Jayprakash%20Somani

ℵ

9 798885 691567

Printed by Libri Plureos GmbH in Hamburg,
Germany